T0064495

A Cluster of Cancers

ALSO BY DR. SHERRY L. MEINBERG

Seizing the Teachable Moment

The Cockroach Invasion

Breadcrumbs for Beginners: Following the Writing Trail

Diabetes ABC

Imperfect Weddings are Best

Recess is Over! No Nonsense Strategies and Tips for Student Teachers and New Teachers

It's All Thought! The Science, Psychology, and Spirituality of Happiness (Teacher's Guide)

Autism ABC

The Bogeyman: Stalking and its Aftermath (TV Premier Episode, Investigation Discovery, 12/12/12)

Toxic Attention: Keeping Safe from Stalkers, Abusers, and Intruders

Be the Boss of Your Brain! Take Control of Your Life

Chicken Soup for the Kid's Soul (Story)

Into the Hornet's Nest: An Incredible Look at Life in an Inner City School

A Cluster of Cancers

A Simple Coping Guide for Patients

DR. SHERRY L. MEINBERG

authorHOUSE®

AuthorHouse™
1663 Liberty Drive
Bloomington, IN 47403
www.authorhouse.com
Phone: 1 (800) 839-8640

© 2015 Dr. Sherry L. Meinberg. All rights reserved.

No part of this book may be reproduced, stored in a retrieval system, or transmitted by any means without the written permission of the author.

Published by AuthorHouse 08/25/2015

ISBN: 978-1-5049-2354-5 (sc)
ISBN: 978-1-5049-2355-2 (e)

Print information available on the last page.

Any people depicted in stock imagery provided by Thinkstock are models, and such images are being used for illustrative purposes only.
Certain stock imagery © Thinkstock.

This book is printed on acid-free paper.

Because of the dynamic nature of the Internet, any web addresses or links contained in this book may have changed since publication and may no longer be valid. The views expressed in this work are solely those of the author and do not necessarily reflect the views of the publisher, and the publisher hereby disclaims any responsibility for them.

DEDICATION

To my personal oncologist, John Paul Brusky, MD, the Head of the Urology Department at Orchard Medical Offices at the Southern California Kaiser Permanente Medical Group, in Downey, who suggested that I write this book: If it weren't for your expertise, I wouldn't be here. I am eternally grateful for the life I continue to live, and for the books I continue to write. Thank you. Thank you. And thank you yet again.

ACKNOWLEDGMENT

I acknowledge with joy and pleasure,
my friend and neighbor,
Barbara Kaye Cooper,
computer whiz extraordinaire
and professional photographer.
Thank you so much for your
selfless help
in times of my need.
You are the best.

CONTENTS

INTRODUCTION

The purpose of *A Cluster of Cancers* is to share experiences and information to promote learning and insight, while offering inspiring support to engage your mind, and help your healing.

INTRODUCTION

Cancer is a word, not a sentence.
—John Diamond, M.D.

As a university supervisor, I was observing a student teacher's high school lesson, when she leaned over and hissed at a boy, "You are a *cancer*. Cancer is *bad!*" Now I ask you, *How does this help?*

Several weeks prior, I had a dangerous and uncertain surgery, in which a five-pound cancerous tumor, along with my totally encapsulated kidney, were removed. (I have a beautiful 9-inch scar, to prove it.) So that young woman's comment rather startled me.

The word cancer has a lot of negative power behind it: people tend to freak out at the very mention of the word. The fear factor is potent. Cancer is frightening to some, and considered a death sentence to others. Whereas, I see a not-so-distant future, in which a cancer prognosis is seen as no more than a pesky fly. After all, polio, diphtheria, and smallpox have been eradicated, while malaria, whooping cough, tetnus, typhoid fever, yellow fever, and several other lesser known diseases are controlled through vaccinations.

Remember leprosy? Historically, there was no cure for it, and lepers were segregated from the population. (In California, in the late 50s, while seniors in high school, my husband's close friend, Marvin, was in love with his sweetheart. And they had plans to marry. They saw each other on a daily basis, and then one day she was simply gone. Vanished. She was found to have Hanson's disease—leprosy—and was immediately whisked away to a leper colony in Florida. She never returned, and Marvin was devastated.) Today, lepers are cured with antibiotics, within a year or two. The future looks just as bright for cancer to join them, as doctors and scientists are working diligently toward that end.

When I was growing up, no one talked openly about cancer, and the word itself was mentioned only in whispers: societal conditioning. The subject was considered so dreadful, so hush-hush, that my brother and I never even knew that our mother had had breast cancer. She had suffered in silence. (And, much later, I couldn't relay such family history to my own cancer doctor, because I didn't know the facts.) We only found out by accident. My brother explained, "The thing with mom was utterly shocking. I walked in on her unannounced. She was standing unclothed from the waist up, staring in the large mirror in her powder room, looking at her bony chest, with horrible, criss-crossed, long scars and missing breasts. I was stunned beyond words, and quickly shut the door. Words fail to convey the feelings with which I was confronted." He was traumatized by the image. She had experienced a radical double mastectomy, and we never knew. (Back then, a lumpectomy wasn't even an option.)

Since then, extraordinary advances have been made against cancer, as shown by the (2014) American Association for Cancer Research Progress Report. The five-year survival rate for *all* cancers has gone from nil, up to 49% (1975-1977), and later 68% (2003-2009). In 2013, cancer deaths really began declining. And now (2014), an astounding 14.5 million Americans with a history of cancer, are still alive! During 2014, the FDA approved six new anticancer therapeutics, alongside new uses for five previously approved anticancer therapeutics, plus two new cancer-imaging agents, and one screening test. And the biomedical research continues.

In the meantime, *A Cluster of Cancers* is meant to make the subject of coping with cancer more easily understandable and simplified, for those not associated with the medical field. Less scary! Knowledge is power.

Granted, in-depth books have been written about most of the common cancers, as well as every single one of the subjects listed in the self-care section. In stark contrast, however, *A Cluster of Cancers: A Simple Coping Guide for Patients* presents an *overview,* as an easy resource guide, kind of like a CliffsNotes summary. (For further in-depth reading, find experts in the field by checking out the reference section—subject by subject.)

You can be a victim of cancer,
or a survivor of cancer.
It's a mindset.
—Dave Pelzer

CANCER DIAGNOSIS

Hope and Hopelessness are both a choice.
Why not choose Hope?
—Greg Anderson

We can all sing along with Bob Seger, "Wish I didn't know now, what I didn't know then." Finding out that you have been diagnosed with cancer is not for the faint-hearted. It is a startling and rude awakening. Upon hearing such unexpected news, many become anxious, freaked out, terrified, paralyzed, or overwhelmed. All feel utterly unprepared.

Having had a number of family members, friends, and neighbors who had experienced cancer, I have now joined their ranks. My response was a tad different, however. Normally, I am cheerful, good-natured, and easy-going. And although I was not thrilled with the report, it wasn't a cataclysmic event for me, as I was more *irritated* than anything else. In the extreme. (Picture steam shooting out of my ears.) Cancer didn't fit into my plans, or my schedule. It simply wasn't a *convenient* time to deal with it. (Ah, the illusion of control! Man plans, God laughs, as the saying goes.) I considered my diagnosis as simply one more hoop to jump through. And I was tired of roadblocks, barriers, and walls. Like me, just think of your diagnosis as an unexpected, *temporary* detour in your life, and roll up your sleeves, and carry on. Consider your cancer situation as simply one more bump in the road of your life.

As such, I invite you to consider your diagnosis another way. Look at the bright side of your predicament: You now have something tangible—cancer—to deal with, instead of something uncertain and nebulous; something to avoid and ignore. Granted, your diagnosis may be daunting, but at the same time, it can actually be *freeing*. You now have a definite goal and purpose; a specific target to aim for: being healthy and cancer-free. (As Lewis Carroll wrote, in *Alice in Wonderland*, "If you don't know where you're going, any road will take you there.") Suddenly, your wholehearted, full-effort focus is in total alignment with healing and well-being, not scattered here, hither, and yon. As such, you can flourish amid the revelation of cancer. Hold that thought.

As Tom Brokaw, the NBC News special correspondent said, when he was diagnosed at 73 with multiple myeloma—an incurable blood cancer: "In about 30 minutes, I went from the illusion of being forever young, to the reality that life has its own way of choosing its own course." Adding, ". . . I was struggling to deal with a strange tug of war between a new reality, and a way of life I could not quite believe was slipping away from me." When he later informed his wife, that he had been given a life expectancy of eight years, he ended with, "This will change our lives." (Understatement of the year!)

I shared with my primary physician that I had been having lower back pain for a couple of years, but thought it was because I kept restraining my back twice a week, hauling a ton of books into and out of the trunk of my car, and to and from the National University where I was lecturing. But, it finally dawned on me that my lower back persistently ached, even when on vacation. (Whereupon, I was informed that *any* symptom that lasts more than a week or two, should be evaluated by a doctor.) As a result, she ordered a battery of tests for me.

Later, I was happily chatting with one of the technicians as she was administering a sonogram. We were laughing and having a lively conversation, when she gazed over at the display screen to check the results, and abruptly stood, and left the room, grim faced. She never returned. I needed no words to tell me that something was wrong. Terribly wrong. Her demeanor said it all. And the next thing I knew, I was scheduled to meet with a urologist, ASAP, which was another clue that cancer was on the horizon.

So the natural questions I wanted to ask my new urologist—John Paul Brusky, M.D.—turned out to be pretty close to those listed by the Mayo Clinic:

*What kind of cancer do I have?
*Where is the cancer located?
*Has it spread?
*Can it be treated?
*What is the chance that my cancer can be cured?
*What other tests or procedures do I need?
*What are my treatment options?

Cancer is not a single condition. It is a general name for well over 200 diseases. The commonality is that each state has abnormal cells that grow and divide in uninhibited ways. Cancer cells generally run amok: they rapidly multiply, invade, and spread. And they do not die within a certain timeframe, as normal cells do. Cancer cells continue to grow, and clump together like grapes, to form a mass of tissue called a tumor. Because of its size and location, the tumor can cause a variety of symptoms and side affects.

The American Cancer Society describes general signs and symptoms that are common with cancers: chronic coughing or hoarseness; difficulty swallowing or a sore throat that won't heal; unexplained pain; persistent fatigue or weakness in muscles and joints; fever and night sweats; unintended or unexplained loss of appetite; weight gain or weight loss; bloating and discomfort after eating; nausea or vomiting; and changes in one's bladder or bowel movements. Other changes to the skin are often signs of cancer: a darkening, or redness, or yellowing of the skin (jaundice), changes in mole appearance (size, shape, or thickness), and sores or wounds that take a long time to heal. And sometimes, a lump or hardened area under the skin will form (breast, testicles, or elsewhere). Or a nagging backache.

The complication is that people, like me, tend to deal with the above issues as separate conditions, instead of seeing them as a collective whole, signifying the greater problem: cancer. And there are others, who display no signs or symptoms at all, until the cancer is well established.

It is important not to assume anything. As Robert A. Nagourney, M.D., says to each of his new patients, "No one is more interested in saving your life than you." This is not the time to be helpless, dependent, and passive. This is not the time to be submissive, because it is out of your area of expertise. Refuse to play the victim role. He goes on to say, "Effective self-advocacy begins with information."

Dr. Anne Wilson Schaef encourages you to "Open new doors and explore options." Do your own research. Ask questions and express your emotions. Don't be embarrassed about asking "dumb" questions. Don't be afraid or hesitate to voice your opinion. Ask, ask, and ask again, until you have the answers you need. Get clear and accurate information, so as to feel confident and comfortable with your choices. "Nothing shapes our lives so much as the questions we ask—or refuse to ask," explains Sam Keen. He urges you to investigate. Think. Deliberate. Evaluate the evidence, and mull it over. "The best prescription is knowledge," says C. Everett Koop, M.D., former U.S. Surgeon General.

After gathering information, it is time to S.T.O.P.—which is a survival situation acronym for Sit, Think, Observe, and Plan, that many groups use in times of emergency. After wise consideration, choose your form of treatment.

Your doctor's appointment may be overwhelming. Upon hearing my diagnosis, my mind was a complete blur. It's a good thing my husband was with me, since I couldn't process much of what my urologist said. To counteract such a response, the American Cancer Society offers tips to make your medical appointments as useful as possible:

*Make a list of questions you want to ask;
*Bring a family member or friend with you, to serve as another pair of ears, to help you remember, and give you support;
*Ask if you can record the conversations;
*Take notes;
*If a word is used that you don't know, asked them to spell it, and explain it; and
*Ask your health team to explain anything you don't understand.

In addition, Anthony Komaroff, M.D.—a physician, a professor at Harvard Medical School, and a newspaper columnist (Ask Dr. K)—has several more suggestions:

*Share all your symptoms and health concerns, even if you think they are unrelated (insomnia, heartburn, etc.);

*Because you may have several doctors for different conditions, bring a list of all your current medications, as well as your vitamins, supplements, and over-the-counter medicines (as they may have negative interactions with your newly prescribed meds). Better yet, throw them all in a bag, for a show-and-tell;

*At the end of your visit, ask for a recap of instructions—a summary of sorts— and check your list, or write them down.

Surgery, chemotherapy, and radiation therapy are the standard procedures for a cancer condition, alongside complementary therapies, or alternative therapy considerations. You can even take part in a clinical trial. (According to the National Cancer Institute, such clinical trials are designed to test new ways to treat cancer, find and diagnose cancer, prevent cancer, manage cancer symptoms or the side effects from treatments.) Understand your options.

Consider the words of Bernie Seigel, M.D.: "Those who survive cancer are those who stay in charge. They are totally involved, knowledgeable, and informed." Participation is key. In days past, no doctors would use the word "cure" in connection with cancer. Now, however, a growing number of doctors are saying that cancer is mostly preventable, manageable, reversible, and curable, but it is up to patients to make the effort.

Understand, however, that, as Tom Brokaw explains: "A particular treatment is not foolproof, or as many medical experts remind us, it is not math, with a fixed and certain outcome." Adding, "The uncertainty of it all is an unwelcome companion." He suggests that you be *confident* that your treatment will work out.

Which is what Phineas "Park" Quimby (1802-1866), Father of the New Thought movement, maintained so long ago. He claimed that medicine and herbs were only effective because of the patient's faith in his or her doctor. And recent research supports his belief, showing that your trust in your physician is far more important than the medicine, treatment, or surgery. Lissa Rankin, M.D., agrees, saying that what your doctor believes matters, and the personality of your physician makes a difference. Choose wisely. Is he or she warm, attentive, and assured? Or brusk, unfeeling, and distant? Note that a caring physician can trigger the self-healing response. Your choice of a doctor is crucial.

I was once assigned to an older doctor who treated me like a kindergartner, even though I had as much knowledge as he (although, admittedly, in another field). He was rude and abrasive and insulted me to the core. I was so upset, I was shaking, and immediately stood up and left. I stormed into the main office, and demanded another doctor, saying, in effect, "He may know his medicine, but he doesn't know how to treat people. He needs a refresher course in Dealing with Patients 101!" I further fumed, "He needs a new and improved attitude!" It turned out that I wasn't the first to demand another doctor. The office staff had heard it all before.

So effective communication skills are a must. Does your doctor enter the room with a smile, call you by name, and sit down at eye-level? Does he or she give you eye contact, or focus on a folder or the computer? Does your doctor listen to you, or does he or she appear to be preoccupied, and do most of the talking? Are you given time to ask questions, or is the doctor constantly checking his or her watch, with a hand already on the doorknob? Do you feel rushed? Consider your long-term commitment.

Suzanne Somers also speaks from experience, when she says, "It is essential to find a doctor who honors your choices, and who will support you fully, throughout your treatment, whatever form it takes." Studies show that those patients with a high level of confidence and trust in their doctor heal faster than the others. Approach all medication and any medical procedure with the relaxed conviction that you have made a good decision for yourself, considering the circumstances. Know that what you expect and believe, you will experience. Your expectations create your reality.

"Life is too short for long pity parties," says Regina Brett, a newspaper columnist, and a New York Times best-selling author of numerous books (in 24 languages), which contain her powerful and humorous insights on being a cancer survivor. "You can get through anything life hands you, if you stay put in the day you are in, and don't jump ahead." She further shares: Each day you have a choice to dwell on the misery of cancer treatments, or look for the joy in simply being alive. Brett found that, "The only day worth living was the one I was in. Those 24 hours were doable, as long as I didn't drag the past and the future into it."

Take heart from the words of Andreas Moritz (author of 14 medical books), quoted in *Knockout*, by Suzanne Somers: "There is no cancer that has not been survived by someone, regardless of how far advanced it was. If even one person has succeeded in healing his cancer, there must be a mechanism for it, just as there is a mechanism for creating cancer."

As Paul Selig wrote, ". . . the cliff that you stand on the edge of is the launching pad for the rest of your life." Think of your cancer as just another experience in your life. Another adventure. Dr. Wayne W. Dyer says that he treated his cancer "diagnosis as *healing information* being given to him, rather than as a disease." See yourself healing your body, mind, and spirit. This does not require Herculean measures. True, some adjustments must be made, and changing some deeply engrained habits may be difficult, but not impossible. Simply determine to make some lifestyle changes, alongside your doctor's suggestions and treatments, while keeping a positive viewpoint.

To paraphrase Marianne Williamson, instead of thinking of your cancer diagnosis as representing a Great End or Armageddon, think of this time as a Great Beginning. She states that: "The only real failure is the failure to grow from what we go through." And she encourages you to: "Make a large leap forward in the actualization of your own potential." You are here to participate.

Doing nothing to help your situation would be ill advised. "Taking responsibility for your life means accepting the reality of your cancer, facing it courageously, then doing what you need to do to heal, learn from it, integrate it, and move on," says Dr. Schaef. See yourself succeeding. As my husband always says, "OUTLAST 'EM!"

The one who asks questions,
doesn't lose his way.
—African Proverb

CANCER STAGES AND GRADING

Staging is the process of finding out
how much cancer there is, and
where it is located.
—American Cancer Society

Cancer is classified into stages. Staging shows how far the cancer has progressed. Various tests are administered to determine the stage of the cancer (physical exams, imaging studies, laboratory tests, pathological reports, and surgical reports). These tests show how large the tumor is, if the cancer cells have spread, and, if so, where they have spread. The National Cancer Institute shows the five main categories that are used for "summary staging" for all kinds of cancer:

*In situ: Abnormal cells are present only in the layer of cells in which they developed

*Localized: Cancer is limited to the organ in which it began, without evidence of spread

*<u>Regional</u>: Cancer has spread beyond the primary site to nearby lymph nodes or tissues and organs

*<u>Distant</u>: Cancer has spread from the primary site to distant tissues or organs or to distant lymph nodes

*<u>Unknown</u>: There is not enough information to determine the stage

Cancer staging has evolved over time, and continues to advance, as doctors and scientists learn more about cancer. Some staging systems cover many different types of cancer, whereas others focus on a particular type. For instance, different staging systems are used for brain and spinal cord cancers, as well as cancers of the blood or bone marrow (lymphomas, leukemia, etc.). The *common* elements considered in most staging systems are listed below:

*Site of the primary tumor and the cell type

*Tumor size and/or extent (reach)

*Regional lymph node involvement (the spread of cancer to nearby lymph nodes)

*Number of tumors (the primary tumor and the presence of metastic tumors, or metastases)

*Tumor grade (how closely the cancer cells and tissue resemble normal cells and tissue)

Grading is a system that shows the characteristics of the cancer cells, which helps your doctor determine the appropriate treatment.

Grading is the description of a tumor
based on how abnormal the cells and tissues
look under a microscope.
—National Cancer Society

CANCER STATISTICS

I don't want to know the odds!
—Han Solo (in *Star Wars*)

The American Cancer Society publishes the expected new cancer cases and deaths each year. In addition it publishes eight regularly updated Cancer Facts & Figures titles, providing the most recent cancer information on specific types in each state, and in the nation. The Internet can readily give such cancer figures and trends, country-by-country, or worldwide.

In 2015, there will be an *estimated* 1,658,370 new cancer cases diagnosed, and 589,430 deaths in the United States. Now I ask you: How does knowing this help *you*? Realize that statistics only measure the past, not the future. And numbers can be manipulated. In the words of Réne Dubos, "Sometimes the more measurable drives out the more important." A reliance on statistics warps many a prognosis. Note that a "hopeless" patient who gets well, when he isn't supposed to, doesn't go back to the doctor," says Bernie S. Siegel, M.D. "Medicine has been studying its failures, when it should have been learning from its successes." He adds that doctors must project hope at all times, as the healing process can often start before the treatment begins. "All patients must be accorded the conviction that they *can* get well, no matter what the odds."

Statistics have nothing to do with you, personally. Ignore them. And remember, too, that a prognosis, is simply an educated guess. So concentrate on your own individual experience, with no comparisons to other cancer patients. This is not a competition. It is your thought and your perspective that counts.

As Alan Cohen maintains: ". . . advisors are making their assumptions on the basis of the statistics of what has happened to others who have gone before you in similar situations. The one factor they cannot calculate is your unique consciousness." Adding: "If you make different mental, emotional, or attitudinal choices, you will create different results." Refuse to be a statistic.

"The most important thing to do is choosing to feel good, regardless of what the numbers on any medical screen might say," advises Dr. Wayne W. Dyer, in *Wishes Fulfilled.* Put it in your head that you will *outlive* any prognosis and any statistic! Believe it! *("I will survive! I will survive and thrive!")* "Simply *choose* to feel good," he adds. A patient of Elisabeth Kubler-Ross, M.D., had the right frame of mind, when she said, "I know that my chances are one in a million, but today I only wish to talk about this one chance."

And speaking of risks and chances, Robert Fulghum shares the following story, in his bestseller, *All I Need to Know I Learned in Kindergarten*:

> When Eli Angel met Rachael, it was love at first sight. Shortly thereafter, he proposed. She turned him down. Why? Because she had cancer; she told him she could not have children, and would not live long. He insisted. He would love her until the end, whenever it came. With love as a shield against impending doom, they married. Love produced four children. And love kept them together in old age.

Your healing requires taking action. Many people have been given a death sentence, and have gone on to lead long and meaningful lives. Greg Anderson, with stage IV cancer, was given 30 days to live. Refusing his prognosis, he went searching for people who were alive and well, who had been labeled "terminal." He has since interviewed *16,000* such cancer survivors (and, in the process, became the Founder and CEO of the Cancer Recovery Foundation International). Determine that you, too, will be one of the survivors. Have a *reason* for living, and you will beat the odds, along with me. Do you want to live to be 100? I'm counting on it.

There are lies, damned lies, and statistics.
—Mark Twain

CANCER CAUSES

Cancer is a complex group of diseases
with many possible causes.
—American Cancer Society

All patients naturally want to know "Why?" Why cancer, why me, why now? Of course, there is not just one cause. There may be physical, mental, and emotional causes, as well as various environmental issues, that trigger cancer. There may be a combination of factors involved. And there may be none that we know of.

"All cancer is caused by chronic inflammation. The number one link to cancer is aging. Cancer below age 40 is a very low risk. It is only after age 50 that it becomes a concern, and at 60 and 70, it increases a lot faster," explains Dr. Russel Blaylock, quoted in Suzanne Somers' *Knockout*.

But no one knows exactly *why* cancers occur. As Gabor Maté, M.D., relates, "As an astute observer has pointed out, . . . attempting to find the cause of cancer on the cellular level is like trying to understand a traffic jam by examining the internal combustion engine." Doctors can point to mitigating factors—medical, environmental, lifestyle, and family history—but no one knows for sure.

The most recent study (January 1, 2015, John Hopkins University School of Medicine), looked at 31 cancer types, and found that the majority, 65 percent, could be explained largely by random mutations—"essentially biological bad luck," said oncologist Dr. Bert Vogelstein, who conducted the study. Co-author, biomathematician Cristian Tomasetti, added that harmful mutations occur for "no particular reason other than randomness." He further added, "It's just because the person was unlucky. It's like losing the lottery." Which makes some patients breathe an enormous sigh of relief, knowing that it wasn't because they were bad, or did something wrong. Cancer is not a punishment.

Traditional cancer doctors view the above "unlucky" study with outright shock and disbelief, citing risky behavior (smoking, unprotected exposure to sunlight), lifestyle (lack of vitamins, ignoring nutritional needs and physical activity), and pollution (plastic, packaged foods, and chemicals in our food, water, and environment). As Anthony Komaroff, M.D., makes plain, in his AskDoctorK newspaper column: "Cancer is not just a matter of bad luck." While Dr. Caroline Myss emphatically states: "No illness develops randomly." She goes on to say, "Your biography becomes your biology."

Some say that everyone has cancer cells in their bodies, but those cells need some sort of trigger to activate them, which goes hand-in-hand with what those touting environmental causes (including our constant exposure to electromagnetic energy from computers, satellite dishes, cell phones, and other such devices), or the physical, mental, emotional, and lifestyle issues as causes for cancer. Once the activation has begun, malignant cells can spread into the surrounding tissue, destroying the surrounding tissue, causing other tumors to develop.

One such cause is championed by those who believe that *all* illness and physical ailments have an emotional component; they see a strong correlation between specific diseases, and the mental/emotional pattern in the person's consciousness that has created the condition. Bernie S. Siegel, M.D., agrees, calling cancer a "disease of the mind." David R. Hawkins, M.D., Ph.D., agrees: "A disease process is evidence that something is amiss in the workings of the mind, and that's where the power to effect a change resides."

Dr. Myss says that ". . . people with cancer often have unsolved connections with the past, unfinished business, and emotional issues." Louise L. Hay also sees character attributes and attitudes that need mending and improving. She says the underlying probable cause for cancer is:

> Deep hurt. Longstanding resentment. Deep secret or grief eating away at the self. Carrying hatreds. A "What's the use?" attitude.

Dr. Wayne W. Dyer shows that every experience in your life, regardless of how you choose to process it at the time, has something extremely valuable to teach you. As such, every tragedy, trauma, illness, injury, or disease can provide a gateway to transformation. So, some people are simply undergoing lessons. As such, there are many who believe that dealing with cancer may be an opportunity for growth.

Sometimes people are wounded because of a defect of character, or a flaw (like self-pity, jealousy, and blame, or the old seven deadly sins of anger, pride, gluttony, greed, vanity, lust, and laziness). Or it may be that their present issues, pressures, and trying times have taken a toll, and their lifestyle is totally out of balance. Or they may need to really take a hard look at their relationships, without the rose-colored glasses, and shed their illusions. (As Robin Norwood says, "Sometimes the most loving thing you can do, is let someone go.")

Many people haul a lot of old baggage around. They desperately hold onto the negative energy that has happened in their lives, never having allowed themselves to release it. They need to deal with this issue.

Cancer is a wake-up call, a jarring shake. There's nothing like a cancer diagnosis to get your attention. If you don't like the identification of the disease, get a second or third opinion. If you don't like the prognosis (the forecasting or prediction), think of it as a *likelihood* (no concrete, no absolute, nothing predestined, or set in stone). You must *believe* that you can deal with cancer successfully. Your cancer may give you an entirely different perspective about your life. You may surprise yourself, by suddenly singing along like Billie Holiday (1921), "There'll be some changes made to-day, there'll be some changes made!" So get on with it. Attend to it. Take the reins, and leave this bump in the road behind. Choose your destiny!

Don't waste your time worrying about "why" or "how" you acquired cancer. Worrying doesn't get things done. Cause or no cause, the minute you are diagnosed, you need to start doing some heavy thinking about your future, and start making lifestyle changes to support your wellness goals.

Take a tip from a kitchen sign: Wishes don't do dishes. Or from an old fisherman's saying: Forty thousand wishes won't fill your bucket with fishes.

And any baker can tell you that recipes don't make cookies. Hopes and dreams and wishes are a waste of your time, effort, and energy. *Action* is what counts: doing, becoming, unfolding, growing, evolving. It is not enough to just stare up the steps; you must step up the stairs. As in walking, so in life: step out, step forward, lengthen your stride, and make your move.

You must actively *participate* in your recovery process. "You're never going to get anywhere if your car is idling in park. Get moving. Take action. Do something toward regaining your health. Deliberately create change." Mike Dooley continues, "Do all you can, with what you have, from where you are, in every direction that feels right." Fully engage yourself, doing anything and everything possible, to see your well-being goals come true. As theoretical physicists, metaphysicians, ministers, priests, rabbis, imams, and other religious leaders tell us: Reality is always open to revision.

We cannot control the wind,
but we have the power
to adjust the sails.
—Chinese Proverb

COPING WITH CANCER

The following suggestions in no way minimize the role of your primary physician, oncologist, or team of cancer professionals. Rather, each section describes how you can *participate*—alongside your treatments—to help regain your health and well-being. Keep an open mind. Use the approaches that make sense to you, and disregard those that don't appeal. Consider the practicality involved. (For instance: Some say that you would have to drink 500 cups of Green Tea a day, to make a difference, whereas others swear by it.) Determine what works for you.

The action points presented for your consideration are meant to relieve a whole level of stress from your cancer experience. Many of the essential points printed herein have been said a number of times, in different ways, by various individuals in all walks of life. The repetition is deliberate. Hearing it several times, in assorted manners, modes, or fashions, gives you a chance to wrap your mind around it, and understand it more thoroughly. Repetition is the basis for learning.

SELF CARE

Being good to oneself
is not selfish,
it is self-preserving.
—Robert S. Cowles III, M.D.

It is said that there is no more important object of attention than your appreciation of self. Herbert Benson, M.D., promotes the idea of the "three-legged stool" of healing. One leg is medication, one leg is surgery and/or other medical treatments, and the third leg is self-care. Your mental, emotional, social, and spiritual health, have a powerful effect on your physical health. Make total wellness your top priority: a way of life.

Now that you have an understanding of the specific cancer you are dealing with—and its cause, risk factors, symptoms, prognosis, treatment, and possible side effects—you can place all of that on the backburner of your mind. See cancer as a challenge, not a threat. "Your body is typically on autopilot to self-heal," Dr. Joseph Mercola reminds us. Now you can directly address your cancer, and focus your energies on the solution. Take personal initiative. Make your own contribution to the situation.

"The quality of your life is determined by what you pay attention to," says Neale Donald Walsch. So turn your attention to recovery, self-care, and your natural state of well-being. As Greg Anderson says, "You must not simply treat illness, you must also treat wellness."

True, cancer will shake the foundations of your normal life. But it can also be a catalyst for deep change. This is not the time for the rending of garments, and the gnashing of teeth. This is not the time to sit and sulk, or to wallow in despair. This is not the time to wring your hands, while moaning the "Oh, woe is me!" blues. Do not simply let the chips fall where they may. *Noooo*. That would be the easy thing to do, but the most irresponsible. Chin up!

See your cancer as an opportunity to learn and grow. The Dalai Lama suggests that you: "Stand back, assess the situation, and arm yourself with as much knowledge as possible." You have a part to play in your recovery. You need to be totally involved. Make peace with your situation, and make the best of it. Think of this period in your life as an extraordinary experience, from which only good can come. See it as self-empowering. Expect the best, and keep moving forward, with a smile on your face, and a song in your heart. *("I am happy regardless of my diagnosis."*)

Lissa Rankin, M.D., says that your body is a reflection of your life experiences. And that the lifestyle choices you make result in the physiological changes in your body. Understand that any addictions you may have, such as tobacco, drugs, and alcohol, will distract you from your healing process. Act accordingly. Dr. Rankin is on "a mission to prove that each facet of how you live your life affects the health of your mind, and with it, the health of your body."

"Taking care of your body is just like taking care of your car. Are you doing the small, regular maintenance checks that keep your engine running smoothly?" asks Chellie Campbell.

Seek solutions. In their book, *All Is Well*, Louise Hay and Mona Lisa Schultz, M.D., advise: "Be open to every healing available, to create health and happiness." Ross Bonander (CancerTreatment.net) shows us that there are five broad categories for Complementary and/or Alternative Cancer Treatment (to which I have added several subjects):

COMPLEMENTARY and/or ALTERNATIVE CANCER TREATMENTS

Ross Bonander

(1) **Biological Approaches**
Vitamins (megavitamin therapy)
Dietary supplements (mushrooms, mistletoe, etc.)
Herbal remedies (green tea, antioxidants, etc.)
Special diets (macrobiotics, phytonutrients, etc.)

(2) **Mind-Body Approaches**
Affirmations
Visualizations
Meditation
Yoga
Tai chi
Hypnosis
Guided Imagery Programs
Relaxation techniques
Music therapy
Art therapy
Humor therapy
Prayer

(3) **Body-Based Approaches**
Massage
Exercises
Reflexology

(4) **Energy-Based Approaches**
Reiki
Healing Touch
Q Gong
Magnetic Field therapy

(5) Ancient Approaches
Traditional Chinese medicine
Ayurvedic medicine
One Spirit medicine (Shamans)
Acupuncture
Acupressure
Aromatherapy

Your personal physician can't come home with you, and hold your hand, saying, "There, there," and tell you what to do. You must take "radical care" of yourself, as Lissa Rankin, M.D., relates. And Bernie S. Siegel, M.D., adds that, "Healing is a creative act, calling for all the hard work and dedication needed for other forms of creativity."

Remember the words of William Shakespeare: "Self-loving is not so vile a sin, my liege, as self-neglecting." Demonstrate that you are in charge of your life, and are willing to act on your own behalf. Engage in more self-care, self-nurturing activities: barber shop/hair salon, facials, make-up, manicures, pedicures, massages, fashions, fun stuff, spas, bubble baths, meditation, and sleep. Pamper yourself. The ball is in your court, and you play a pivotal role in your healing and recovery. Simply be open and willing to make some changes to benefit your health and well-being. ("*I nurture and support myself.*") Involve your entire being in the *idea* of being healthy.

Alan Cohen says that the greatest gift you can give yourself is the precious gift of self-care. A helpful suggestion by Greg Anderson, in *The Cancer Conqueror*, is to think of that part of you that has cancer, as your inner child. Then your task becomes centered on taking care of your child, and nurturing your child back to health, helping your inner child to conquer cancer.

All the experts give the same advice: Do some good self-mothering. Feed yourself in the manner of chicken soup, drink more water than sodas, use less sugar and salt, pace yourself, nurture yourself, take supplements, rest, and get some daily exercise and fresh air. Experts suggest that you avoid artificial sweeteners altogether. Brendon Barnum—President and CEO, Longevity Labs—writes in his foreword for *Put Old On Hold,* by Barbara Morris, R.Ph., that how you choose to live from day to day is the key: "Simple changes in diet, exercise, stress relief, and nutritional supplementation, can add years to your life, and life to your years." You can improve your health one day at a time. See yourself as healthy.

And it's good to know: "Making a healthy shift in any one component of your life will have a positive influence on your entire state of well-being," as both Deepak Chopra, M.D., and David Simon, M.D., tell us. Remember: slow and steady wins the race.

Self-nurturing and self-caring is not self-indulgence. It is self-preservation: being responsible, and not allowing any excuses. If you are electing to have surgery (as I did), having a Living Will and a Health Care Proxy, or power of attorney in place, will alleviate concerns for yourself, as well as your family. Both are advance directives—written and legally binding documents—in which you describe what kind of medical care you hope to receive (or don't want!), if a serious accident or illness renders you unable to communicate. Otherwise, a relative or court-appointed guardian—who does not know your wishes—may be asked to make medical decisions for you. If your wishes aren't known, family conflicts may ensue. (Surely, you've seen such situations played out in the media, when comatose celebrities' families are divided regarding treatments, causing clashes and delays. Not to mention lawyers and courts.) You don't want that. Experts say that the younger you are, the higher the risk, and the more you have at stake.

For example: My next-door neighbor was recently whisked to the hospital, and after an emergency operation, he contracted pneumonia, and slid into an unexpected comma. He was finally given Last Rites. The family and his doctors were at odds as to how to handle the situation, when he suddenly awoke. You just never know . . .

"Give your physical well-being a high priority," suggests Victoria Moran. "Healthy people do healthy things." Look out for yourself. It is said that there is no more important object of attention than that of your appreciation of self.

Indeed. Dr. Eldon Taylor says, ". . . just as with doing your own breathing, you must do what is necessary yourself." Treat yourself as the most important person in your life! Now is the time to tend to yourself first (fasten your seatbelt, as the airlines direct, and apply the oxygen mask to yourself before helping others).

"True self-care enhances your ability to care for others," says Alan Cohen. All first responders—firefighters, police, and medical personnel—as well as parents and teachers, also take care of others by taking care of themselves first. Take the words of Gilda Radner to heart: "It is important to realize that you have to take care of yourself, because you can't take care of anybody else until you do." And Dr. Alberto Villoldo asks: "How can you not attend to your own healing if you care about your fellow beings?" Find the balance between caring for yourself and caring for others.

Attend to your own joy and happiness. Focus on taking great care of yourself. "Putting yourself first does not mean being what you term 'selfish'—it means being self-aware," explains Neale Donald Walsch. Preventative maintenance is key. Find what works for you. Stop ignoring your needs. Recognize that you don't have to have talent or education to take that first step. Begin by adoring and appreciating your body. Louise L. Hay says, "Self love is the most important gift you can give yourself."

Regina Brett is quoted as saying, "Cancer taught me to stop saving things for a special occasion. Every day is special. You don't have to get cancer to start living life to the fullest. My post-cancer philosophy? No wasted time. No ugly clothes. No boring movies." And she continues on in the same vein: "Cancer is a great wake-up call. A call to take the tag off the new lingerie and wear that black lacy slip. To open the box of pearls, and put them on. To use the fireplace. To crack open the bath oil beads before they shrivel up in a bowl on the toilet tank. To light the candles." She further suggests that you walk out of boring movies, and close any book that doesn't dazzle you. Pamper yourself. Treat yourself as the most important person in your life. Accept and love yourself unconditionally. And remember the words of Elisabeth Kubler-Ross, M.D.: "The only thing I know that truly heals people is unconditional love."

Whatever minor indulges you choose,
their payoff is more energy,
both physical and emotional.
—Victoria Moran

MIND/EMOTIONS

There is no illness of the body
apart from the mind.
—Socrates

At long last, science is finally recognizing what Hippocrates (460-370 BC—who did the earliest known work on cancer) and Socrates (469/70-399 BC—one of the founders of Western philosophy) said so long ago: There is no separation between body and mind. Your mind and emotions play a crucial role in your health. Many ancient healing systems emphasized the interconnection between thoughts and emotions in healing the body, and current scientific research (from the fields of psychology, neuroscience, endocrinology, medicine, sociology, and even computer science) are proving the staggering power you have over your own health. Your mind controls your body. When you hold a positive belief and expectation of your body's health, alongside that of showering yourself with nurturing care, you can live a long and vital life.

"Ailments are largely the result of negative emotions," says Dr. Masaru Emoto. "The condition of the mind has a direct impact on the condition of the body." And Christiane Northrup, M.D. concurs: "Diseases don't just appear out of nowhere." She explains, "Old emotions (grief, anger, and shame) can cause disease." Adding: "Your emotions have to shout louder and louder—often through physical symptoms—in order to get your attention."

Father Paul Keenan says that many "chronic headaches, back pains, and other ongoing complaints are due to the emotional baggage we are carrying around with us." Furthermore, he states in his book, *Good News for Bad Days*, that ". . . some life-threatening diseases, such as cancer and heart attacks, are due to severe emotional distress." And Dr. Emoto adds that, "The importance of being positive cannot be underestimated."

Understand that your body is naturally wired to heal itself, but your mind operates this healing system. Emotion is the driving force behind motivation, positive or negative. You can think yourself sick, or you can think yourself well. Know that your positive thoughts and emotions help your body to repair itself. Your genes are not fixed in cement. Epigenetics proves that your genes are actually fluid, flexible, and highly influenced by your environment. Know that your lifestyle choices (diet, exercise, relationships, positive or negative thoughts, stress management, self-talk, beliefs, emotions and behaviors) literally affect your DNA. And those same cancer lifestyle risks are all under your control. Simple adjustments in your lifestyle can improve your health.

". . . what's missing for most of us is any focus on ongoing, daily, emotional self-care," declares Dr. Candice B. Pert. "We tend to deal with the physical aspects of keeping ourselves healthy and ignore the emotional dimension—our thoughts and feelings, even our spirits, our souls." Understand that all your emotional upheaval will eventually wear yourself out.

The tendency to ignore your emotions is yesterday's thinking, Dr. Pert continues. "Emotions are a key element in self-care." In her book, *Molecules of Emotion*, she cites Caroline Sperling, who states that ". . . people get cancer by burying their emotions, denying and repressing them." All such individuals can identify with Woody Allen, who once said, "I can't express anger. That's my problem. I internalize everything. I just grow a tumor instead." (Me, too. I grew four fibroids, as large as oranges, and a five-pound cancer tumor. Later, I finally realized that by not releasing my anger, blame, and resentment, I was letting it fester, and harming my own body.) And Dr. Marc E. Lippman agrees, saying, "The chronic psychological status of the individual may play an important role in facilitating tumor promotion. . ."

Which is exactly what Louise L. Hay maintains in her popular book, *Heal Your Body* (1976, with numerous reprints thereafter), showing that every illness is affected by specific emotional factors. Since then, experts and scientific studies have supported her claims, showing that specific emotions release certain chemicals in response. Neale Donald Walsch, in Book 1 of his *Conversations with God* series, also shows that "All illness is self-created," though quite unconsciously, through your habits and emotions. Such as:

*Hate is an intense hostility or dislike, that is deeply destructive, and poisons the body;

*Worry is considered to be the worst form of mental activity, next to hate. It is not only pointless, but wasted energy. (Abraham-Hicks agrees: "Worrying is using your imagination to create something you don't want.") It creates bio-chemical reactions which harm the body, producing all kinds of health issues; and,

*Fear is worry magnified. It causes a change in brain and organ function, and ultimately a change in behavior. (Note: A strong fear of cancer negatively affects the healing process.)

Hate, anger, worry, and fear are like a fisherman's hook, says the Dalai Lama. "Ensure that you are not caught up by those hooks." Mark Twain correctly observed, that: "Anger is an acid that can do more harm to the vessel in which it is stored than to anything on which it is poured." And Dr. Carolyn Myss agrees: "Anger, bitterness, rage, and resentment, handicap the healing process, or abort it completely." She further explains that ". . . the energy of vengeance is one of the most toxic emotional poisons to your biological system, causing all kinds of dysfunctions."

While, Paul Selig shows that, "If you elect to stay in a place of blame, you continue to tether yourself to the person you want to blame, and bind yourself to your history." To which, Dr. Myss adds: "Remaining attached to negative events and beliefs is toxic to our minds, spirits, cell tissue, and lives." All show that you need to release the past in order to move on with your lives. She stresses that, "Healing begins with the repair of emotional injuries." And that, "Healing requires unity of mind and heart."

Neale Donald Walsch continues: "All illness is created first in the mind." He goes on to say that hate, worry, blame, and fear—together with their offshoots: anxiety, bitterness, impatience, unkindness, judgmentalness, resentment, and condemnation—all attack the body at the cellular level. He believes that it is *impossible* to have a healthy body under these conditions. He further states that even those patterns of a lesser degree—like conceit, self-indulgence, and greed—can lead to physical illness, or a lack of well-being.

Gabor Maté, M.D., offers the same idea, in his book, *When the Body Says No: Exploring the Stress Disease Connection* (published in fifteen languages). "Cancer, like other diseases, represents far more than a purely physical process. Its onset, biology, and outcomes are inseparable from a person's history, relationships, life stresses, and emotional states." Adding that, "Shame is the deepest of the 'negative emotions.'"

In *All is Well* (2013), Louise L. Hay and co-author Mona Lisa Schulz, M.D., suggest that you take a look at what your body is telling you about the connection between your behavior and your health. The higher states of mind and emotion are those of love, goodness, understanding, cheerfulness, joyfulness, friendliness, caring, helpfulness, and so on, and they are the ones to cultivate, in order to live a long, healthy life. Deepak Chopra, M.D., reiterates that positive emotions, such as love, compassion, courage, faith, and hope, have a healthy, life-supporting outlook on life, causing you to live as many as ten years longer. Good to know. Robert Arnot, M.D., urges you to pledge to develop your emotions to benefit yourself, your family, and those around you.

In another of his books, *The Only Thing That Matters,* Neale Donald Walsch highlights the idea that your emotions are chosen. "They are selected exactly the way you select the clothes you want to wear. Emotions are the costumes of the Mind. The Mind *decides* to feel a certain way." He goes on to say that if you "*change* your Thought about something (cancer), you create a different Emotion around it—which will produce a different Experience of it."

"Real self-responsibility means that you're 100 percent accountable for the quality of your life. You're in charge of your thoughts and emotions and the outcomes you create," states Sandra Anne Taylor. And your positive thoughts lead to self-healing, says Lissa Rankin, M.D. Blaming your condition will only serve to heighten its existence. Make the most of your situation. Alan Cohen says, "Courage means that you feel fear, but move ahead anyway." Find a way to be happy *now,* with cancer, on your way to becoming cancer-free. Turn your attention to where you want to be: healthy. Celebrate your freedom to choose your emotional state.

All illness and physical ailments
have an emotional component.
—Christiane Northrup, M.D.

SELF-TALK

When your self-talk changes,
so does the reality you experience.
—Dr. Eldon Taylor

Pay close attention to how you talk to yourself. Your words have enormous energy and power. Know that your self-talk is critical. "That voice inside your head has a huge impact on who you are and how you live your life," says Belinda Anderson. It is clear that the types of words you think and speak can alter your expectations and your perception of reality. "Watch what you give your attention to. Watch what comes out of your mouth," advises Rev. Deborah L. Johnson.

Understand that how you think about and talk about yourself and your cancer is key. In her book, *Every Word Has Power*, Dr. Yvonne Oswald cites a study by Dr. Raymond L. Birdwhistell (1970), proving ". . . that the words you speak to others represent just seven percent of the results you get from your communication. The words you speak to yourself, however, generate 100 percent of the results you'll get in your life." Alan Cohen agrees, suggesting: "Stay alert to your tendency to use words couched in victimization or disempowerment."

Get that "Poor, Poor, Pitiful Me" song (by Warren Zevon) out of your head. Banish the inner voice that whimpers and whines, *It's not fair! Why me? Why now?* Fight against using cancer as fuel for self-pity. Rise above this character flaw. It is a negative indulgence, a seductive excuse, that can easily become habitual. Make your mantra: No sniveling! And soldier on. Self-pity is said to be more harmful to you than any of your physical conditions. As Maya Angelou said, "Self-pity in its early stages is as snug as a feather mattress. Only when it hardens does it become uncomfortable." Your mind creates your experience. You need to express your negative emotions, and get them out of your system. Otherwise, they stay and clump together inside your body, which harms you. Silence your excuses and distractors. Suspend self-criticism.

Make yourself a higher priority: Number One. Get to know yourself. ("Three things extremely hard: steel, diamonds, and getting to know one's self." Ben Franklin.) Let go of the need to care for others to the exclusion of your own wants, needs, and development. Practice self-love, self-forgiveness, self-compassion, and self-understanding. Make decisions that are in your own best interests. Consider the philosophy of

Groucho Marx: "I take care of me. I am the only one I've got." Be good to yourself.

You are not only what you think, feel, and say about yourself but what you believe about yourself, says Barbara Hoberman Levine, in her book, *Your Body Believes Every Word You Say.* And Deepak Chopra adds that doctors now say that every single cell in your body is vitally aware of how you think and feel about yourself.

Dr. Carolyn Myss states that, "Belief in yourself is required for healing." And, unfortunately, the words of your inner dialogue are often skewed toward the negative ("I'm not good enough," "I'm a failure," "Poor me," "This is so unfair," and so forth). Such words are unproductive and destructive, increasing your stress level, while eroding your sense of worth. Understand that your constant mental chatter, though subtle, is an extremely powerful form of energy, drawing like affects to you. This repeated negativity can destroy any seed of hope that you may otherwise have. "If you realized how powerful your thoughts are, you would never think a negative thought," said Mildred Norman Ryder (AKA: Peace Pilgrim). The therapeutic community estimates that it is necessary to have positive-to-negative self-comments on a ratio of at least five-to-one to be healthy.

"Chronic thoughts about unwanted things invite, or ask for, matching experiences," says Esther Hicks. Or, as Lissa Rankin, M.D., succinctly puts it: "Think sick, Be sick." Focus on what you *do* want. If you feel overwhelmed, and say, "I can't deal with my cancer;" "I can't handle it," or "It's too difficult," more than likely, you can't. You are creating resistance. You are limiting yourself at the get-go. Know that your subconscious mind hears you, and more importantly, *believes* what you say, setting out to make it happen. You sabotage yourself, shooting yourself in the foot. Negative self-talk means that you are disallowing your expansion, and leads to a self-fulfilling prophecy. Realize that your self-talk creates your reality. Deliberately choose your thoughts.

Instead of seeing your cancer as difficult, think of it as a *challenge;* think of it as an *opportunity.* Instead of thinking of cancer as a problem, work towards a *solution.* Instead of focusing on how horrible your cancer is, start focusing on how wonderful your health is. Your internal dialogue counts! See your cancer as only a bump in the road of your looong life. See your cancer as something to confront, deal with, and ultimately discard. Control the direction of your thought. As Elizabeth Scott, M.S., says, "Turn self-sabotage into self-mastery." Are you moving forward, or are you standing still?

"Use your inner speech to stay focused on what you intend to create," says Dr. Wayne W. Dyer, in *The Power of Intention.* Change your negative self talk to the positive *("I can do this!" "I am successful." "I am strong. I am fit. I am healthy." "I am cancer-free!" and so forth).* Fill your mind with positive images and thoughts. Think of them as emotional Kevlar to counteract the negativity. *("I am healing. My body is healing. I am healing now.")* Practice makes perfect. Keep positive. *("My health is getting better and better and better!")* As your self talk changes for the better, so too, does the reality you experience.

Your own words are the bricks and mortar
of the dreams you want to realize.
Your words are the greatest power you have.
The words you choose and their use
establish the life you experience.
—Sonia Croquette

DECIDE/DECLARE

It is your decisions,
and not your conditions,
that determine your destiny.
—Anthony Robbins

Granted, your cancer diagnosis may have come out of left field, and blindsided you, but it's your life, your body, and your health, so take responsibility for it. Choose to make the best of this difficult situation. You can't remain mired in the muck forever. Now is the time to decide. Both big and little decisions are involved with your choice of cancer treatment (surgery, chemotherapy, radiation, complementary, or alternative cancer therapies), as well as your self care and coping considerations. It is not for the chicken-hearted. It takes guts, and it takes courage, but nothing will happen until *you* make a decision. You can no longer be safe sitting on the fence. Take a stand. Make a commitment. Promise yourself to work toward good health and wellness.

Sure, you may be riddled with fear, anxiety, and uncertainty. You may be discouraged and filled with doubts, because of the risk involved. (Remember what William Shakespeare said: "Our doubts are traitors.") It is a scary situation. You may feel overwhelmed. But you must make a decision. Get past the trauma and drama. Refuse to be stuck in the quagmire of negativity. Decide not to give up. Stand your ground. Listen to your doctors' recommendations, and your family's suggestions, while doing your own research. Think twice, and think again. Take a few deep breaths before agreeing with anyone about anything. Be responsible. The sooner you make a choice, the sooner your recovery will become evident.

Now is the time to decide. Make the most life-enhancing choice. Now is the time to make a commitment. Bob Proctor says that you must "Clear out all the *hopefully*, and *maybe*, and *can't*, from your mind." This is not the time to whine and say, "I'll try." You must get beyond the idea of trying. True, trying may get you headed in the right direction, but you must know in your bones, and know in your soul, that you *will* be cancer-free again. "Dare to believe in a possibility you've never seen," says Rev. Deborah L. Johnson. "Claim with all your heart of hearts, your deepest desire." Determine to be healthy and strong again. Know that it is so! Step forward. "Own it, claim it, bless it, and be thankful for it," says Neale Donald Walsch. "Don't 'try' to do anything. Do it." Yoda said it another way (in *Star Wars*, Episode V, *The Empire Strikes Back*): "Do or do not . . . There is no try." Consistently work towards your wellness goal. Declare with certainty that you will be healthy and cancer-free. Choose life.

Hunter Doherty "Patch" Adams, M.D., agrees, saying: "When you left the house today, you had the intention of putting clothes on, and you did. You didn't *try* to put your pants on today. You simply put them on. The same has to hold for all of our intentions. We don't try to be more loving partners. We make the intention, and we act on it."

"Many physicians would agree that all healing depends upon the patient's inner decision to release the problem to solution," says Dr. Carolyn Godschild Miller, a clinical psychologist. It is time for some introspection, and self-discovery. It is time to review your life. It is not enough to know what you need to do. The tough part is actually doing it. "With each decision you make, and every thought you think, you are creating your future right now," explains Bob Proctor. "Decisions are actually a direct reflection of who you are, and where your purpose is. Each one confirms the beliefs you have about yourself, and the direction you are traveling," he continues.

As you no doubt have heard: Change your thinking, and change your world! Look at your situation in a fresh way. See your cancer as a creative challenge, not a burden. Place your personal spin on it, by dealing with your lifestyle issues in your own way. Make changes that appeal to you. Stretch yourself beyond your usual routine.

("I act in healthy ways.") Decide to be well. Decide to be in perfect health. Commit to it. Focus on it. As the old expression goes: Show me a ten-foot wall, and I'll show you an eleven-foot ladder. Determine to be cancer-free.

Once you make your decision to be healthy, and work toward a wellness lifestyle, know it! State it! Declare it! Announce it! Express it! *("I am healthy. I am well.")* And accept that it has already happened. Louise L. Hay says, "Every day, declare what you want in life. Declare it as though you have it!" And Marianne Williamson agrees, saying, "If you want a miracle, you have to *claim* it!"

There is tremendous energy in your spoken words. Once you declare that something is so, you send a signal out into the universe to move that choice toward you. Whatever you command comes to be. You attract it. You magnetize it. Stake your claim. Decide and declare. Declare it with absolute certainty. State your declaration aloud, with *feeling*, and allow it to come into your life. Picture Scarlett O'Hara, in *Gone with the Wind* (by Margaret Mitchell), when she shakes her fist at the heavens, and shouts, "As God is my witness, I'll never be hungry again!" Now *that's* a declaration! Proclaim something like it: "As God is my witness, I'll be totally healthy, again!"

Once you make a decision,
the universe conspires to make it happen.
—Ralph Waldo Emerson

BELIEF

The thing always happens
that you really believe in,
and the belief in a thing makes it happen.
—Frank Lloyd Wright

"Beliefs control biology!" Bruce H. Lipton, Ph.D., enthusiastically states in his groundbreaking book, *The Biology of Belief*, which clearly shows that the mind overrides the body. He is a former medical school professor and research scientist. His experiments, and those of other scientists, show that your genes and DNA do not control your biology; that it is your positive and negative thoughts that control your biology (when patients *believe* the treatment works, it does, whether it is a real drug, or just a sugar pill). He further says that "Your beliefs act like filters on a camera . . . and your biology adapts to those beliefs." Your beliefs are that powerful.

Believing in yourself is required for healing. Believe that you can make it through your cancer process; that you have the confidence, dedication, and willingness to pursue your goals; that you can remain motivated, and stay the course. Lissa Rankin, M.D., adds that, from the onset, hold the belief that: "It's all going to be okay." So believe in your recovery, in spite of appearances.

Adding fuel to the flame is a quote from *Science News*, ". . . beliefs are as powerful a physical influence on the brain as neuroactive drugs," said Dr. Read Montague, Director of the Computational Psychiatry Unit at the Virginia Tech Carilion Research Institute. As such, Dean Graziosi adds, "Like an outdated computer, we need to upgrade our beliefs and our way of thinking. You are in control. It's time for you to purge your limiting beliefs, and substitute them with more supportive, empowering, *limitless beliefs*."

After you have made your cancer treatment decision, and committed to it, it does no good to question your conclusion, or second-guess yourself: "Is this medication really effective?" "Is this treatment really the right process for me?" "Is this surgery really necessary?" Such questions are detrimental to your progress. You must *believe* that you have chosen the best treatment for yourself. Stick with it. Don't flip-flop back and forth. Otherwise, you are unintentionally working at cross-purposes. Don't let your unconscious ambivalence interfere with your healing.

In your mind, refuse to see the cancer condition. Neal Donald Walsch says to be prepared to ignore the evidence of your own eyes, and close your ears to anything of the contrary, and refuse to consider any negative outcome. Focus instead upon your total and complete health. You must know—absolutely *know*—in advance, that you will be cancer-free. See your body's perfection. Believe with conviction that it is so. See your perfect state.

Dr. Eldon Taylor says, in his book, *I Believe: When What You Believe Matters*: "The power of belief, the absolutely awesome incredible power of belief, is the genie in your life. Let me say that again: The absolutely awesome and incredible power of your belief is the genie in your life." Be constantly, relentlessly optimistic. Believe in positive results.

"It's completely irrelevant why you believe what you believe," says Mike Dooley, in *The Top Ten Things Dead People Want to Tell You*, "however logical or illogical it may be, prudent or reckless, conservative or aggressive, self-serving or altruistic; that you *believe* is sufficient for manifestation." He goes on to say that, ". . . the one who so believes—not just claims to believe, but *truly* believes—without contradiction . . . will, according to her own beliefs, survive" cancer or amass a fortune, or write an award-winning novel. Whatever.

Believing involves acting, speaking, and thinking. Your belief, certainty, and faith, are necessary and powerful forces for creating a healthy life. Your belief shapes your reality. Everything you experience is directly linked to what you believe. You are only limited by your beliefs. Heal your thoughts, and your body will follow. *Feel* gratitude and appreciation, as if your desires and prayers have already been answered. From the start, hold the belief that you have chosen the right treatment, and that you are in remission. Expect to get better. Choose wellness.

Numerous authors and lecturers, from all professions, agree with Shakti Gawain, when she says that you always attract into your life whatever you ". . . think about the most, believe in most strongly, expect on the deepest levels, and imagine the most vividly." You have to believe it, before you see it, as explained by Dr. Wayne Dyer, author of 16 New York bestsellers, in his book, *You'll See It When You Believe It.*

Your thoughts are seeds that you are always planting, as Joan Gattuso explains: "Just as apple seeds produce apple trees, and tomato seeds produce tomato plants, so too do thoughts you place in your mind produce after their kind. You don't plant cactus seeds and expect to produce a gardenia. Nor do you plant seeds of bitterness and expect to produce loving kindness. Thoughts held in mind produce after their kind."

Know that the beliefs you hold create the results you manifest. You have the potential for self-induced healing built into you. Your body responds to your thought patterns. Your body reacts to all your thoughts, words, and actions. Your body believes every word you say (which is also the title of a book by Barbara Levine), and is naturally wired to heal itself, but your mind operates this self- healing system.

Believe that cancer remission is already yours. Believe in a self-fulfilling prophesy of glowing health. Believe that you are worthy of having what you want. Believe that you are able to have what you want. Have unwavering faith. Know that it is so. Expect it. Know that your expectations determine your outcomes. Your expectations make all the difference. Mike Dooley says, in *Even More Notes from the Universe*, that ". . . expectation unlocks wheels, parts seas, moves mountains, and changes everything." Fixate on what you want to create, says Alan Cohen. Anticipate the best.

"Healing is a process, not an event," explains Dr. Anne Wilson Schaef. Understand that it is common for patients to begin to lean in the direction of recovery, only to stop and fretfully check to see if they've veered off course, somehow. Then, when they think they are not getting better, or not making fast enough progress, they offer resistant thoughts, which makes them lose the improved ground they had gained. (Like ripping off a Band-Aid and picking at a scab.) Mike Dooley says, in *Manifesting Change*, "Never trust appearances." He goes on to say, "Just because you can't see the progress you're making doesn't mean you aren't making any." And Dr. Schaef adds, "One cannot push the process of healing," Or, as Judith Orloff, M.D., reminds us, "There is no way to hurry a rose to bloom."

Sandra Anne Taylor explains: "The work you're doing now is setting down roots equal to the size of your success." Be like a farmer eager for the new crop, who knows that any rush to harvest will spoil the yield, says Mike Dooley in *Even More Notes From the Universe.* (Do not dig up the dirt, to see if the seed is sprouting!) Understand that progress is to be measured in your mind, not in inches or yards, blocks or miles, minutes or hours, days or weeks, seasons or years. "Make time your friend," Elisabeth Kubler-Ross, M.D. urges.

Know and *believe* that you are healing. Embrace the idea that you are gaining ground, whether you can actually see it, or not. Hang in there. As William Feather said, "Success seems to be largely a matter of hanging on after others have let go." Hold onto the belief that your treatments are working. Positive expectations are crucial.

Neale Donald Walsch says, "Be aware of the process unfolding, and quietly know that everything is going to be okay with you." Don't worry as to why it is taking so long. Your success is in your head; it is how you see it. Understand that your cancer took a long time to form, and it will take some time to heal. There is no quick-fix solution to cancer. Have patience. Anticipate the best.

Consider the words of UCLA's wildly popular basketball coach, John Wooden, on how to make change happen: "Don't look for the big, quick improvement. Seek the small improvements one day at a time. That's the only way it happens—and when it happens, it lasts." Give your body a chance to improve. It took a long time for your cancer to form, so give it time to heal. *Know* that your body is healing, and let it go at that. Trust that it *will* happen, and be at peace. Anticipate the best.

Understand that the thoughts you tell yourself, and the words you speak, create your experiences. How you think and talk to yourself determines your achievement. Jack Canfield observed, "It is a universal principle that you get more of what you think about, talk about, and feel strongly about." Your thoughts become the things and events of your life. Your unconscious mind accepts whatever you choose to believe. *("I am skinny. I am bald. I am ugly. I am going to die from cancer.")* Your feelings and beliefs impact every cell in your body. How you speak to yourself matters.

Literally hundreds of experts and books, quoted by past and present-day authors, agree that a strong belief makes things happen. Believe, know, and feel your body's capacity to change. Expectation is a powerful force. Know that your expectations and thoughts influence your health. Scientific data shows that you can radically alter your body's physiology just by changing your mind. When you change your thoughts, and change your beliefs, you change your biochemistry. Your positive thoughts and feelings help your body repair itself. See yourself as cancer-free and healthy, regardless of current circumstances. Confidently believe the best for yourself. ("*I am healthy. I am strong. I am beautiful. I am cancer-free.*") Hold that thought. Dwell on the end result. ("I am totally healthy, inside and out." "*I live a long, healthy, active life.*" "*I am filled with vim, vigor, and vitality.*") Work towards a wellness lifestyle. Believe in the possibility of meaningful, substantial, and sustainable change!

Everything is possible
to the extent that you are certain.
—David Cameron Gikandi

ACT AS IF

The only way we truly make a decision is by acting.
—Dan Millman

Over 100 years ago, Dr. William James said, "If you want a quality, act as if you already have it." He suggested that you adopt the manner, facial expressions, posture (and so forth), and you will soon get the feelings associated with what you want.

Research shows that if you walk around with a forced smile long enough, you'll ultimately find yourself cheering up. Loretta LaRoche says that if you force yourself to walk with long strides, swinging your arms and holding your head up high, with a big smile on your face, you'll feel more powerful and engaged in life, than if you shuffle along, dragging your feet, dangling your arms like a gorilla, and staring at the ground. She states, "*Creating* the motion *triggers* the emotion." Taking such positive action is a simple form of self-suggestion. Fake it 'til you make it. Confidence brings success.

Know that you play a significant role in the outcome of your cancer experience. Involve your entire being in the *idea* of being healthy. In your mind's eye, see, feel, and act as if your well-being is already accomplished. *("I feel healthy, and I am healthy.")* Your imagination is powerful. Your beliefs are powerful. Believing in yourself, and seeing yourself as cancer-free, is a large part of making the transition to *being* cancer-free. Simply imagine it, and hold that thought. Believe it is so, with a total lack of doubt. Act as if you are living your life on purpose. Keep your sights on your cancer-free goal. Be fully engaged. Persistence can compensate for many shortcomings.

Behave as if your success is inevitable, suggests Mike Dooley, in *Manifesting Change*. Act as if you are totally healthy, inside and out, and you will draw it to you. Pay attention, act on what you know, and move on. Consciously create your experience of health. *Be* health. Your intention becomes your reality. Be tougher than cancer.

Accept the tenet that you are already healed, says Gregg Braden. Act the part. Act as if your cancer-free dreams have come true. Act as if it is a done deal. Act as if you are already cancer-free and healthy. Think, feel, and act as if, without hesitation. Mike Dooley says that ". . . the absolute fastest way to manifest change is to claim that you already have it." Acting as if is belief in motion.

Marianne Williamson speaks of a Talmudic principle: "In the midst of the darkest night, we should act as if the morning has already come." Conduct yourself with concrete confidence. I continued writing my manuscript, *Autism ABC*, during my bout with cancer, with an inner knowing that the book would be finished, and published. I did not let any doubts dissuade me from my goal.

In a "Prepare for the worst, and pray for the best" mode, I was advised to get my affairs in order. So, on the off-chance, I updated my Living Will, as well as my Health Care Proxy, and discussed the details of my insurance and mortuary plot with my husband. However, as a university student teacher supervisor, I carried on, as normal. I refused to tell anyone at work of my upcoming operation, as I didn't want to see any sad faces, or hear any "Oh, woe," or "Poor you," and other such comments, alongside disaster stories. I was determined to carry on as usual. I only wanted to be surrounded with positive thoughts, feelings, and laughter. And I knew beyond a shadow of a doubt, that I would survive. And I did, of course (although it was touch-and-go, I later found out). Thereafter, I returned immediately back to work, with no one the wiser. As Barbara Morris, R. Ph., suggests, "Act with educated fearlessness."

Note: "You are not 'in denial' when you recognize a problem and behave normally in spite of it. There is a difference between having a problem in your life and making a problem of your life," explains Victoria Moran. Maintain the conviction that all is well in your life. And act it. Understand that each action you take is a physical demonstration of your mental belief in your health and well-being. "Act as though you are healthy, and you will be," said Ernest Holmes, in his book, *The Science of Mind*. "There is no limitation."

The largest question facing the human race
is not when will you learn,
but when will you act on what you have learned?
—Neale Donald Walsch

STRESS MANAGEMENT

When life kicks you,
let it kick you forward.
—Kay Yow, Cancer Fund Founder

You may feel a great deal of stress upon hearing the diagnosis of cancer. True, you may feel that this situation came out of left field, and that you have no control over it. But there is now strong evidence to show that prolonged stress can negatively affect your health, and that the stress response can cause cancer. As such, you need to get a handle on it. Now.

Stress is considered to be any physical, chemical, or emotional factor that causes bodily or mental unrest. An important goal for you is the management of your life stresses. Understand that when you are in the middle of a stress response, your body's self-maintenance and self-repair functions come to a screeching halt. And repetitive stress responses progressively break down your body, producing headaches, an upset stomach, back pain, and trouble sleeping. Dr. Kelly A. Turner, in her book *Radical Remission*, cites a landmark stress study, published in *the New England Journal of Medicine* (1991), showing that stress weakens your immune system (which plays a key role detecting and removing cancer cells from your body), making it harder to deal with your cancer.

'It is not just stress, but the way of reacting to stress, that makes a difference in the susceptibility to disease," says O. Carl Simonton, M.D., in *Getting Well Again*. Some people try to relieve their stress through excessive smoking, drinking, overeating, and using illicit drugs. Some simply shut down. (One woman who worked in the room next to me, upon hearing that she had cancer, refused to make small talk with anyone. She wouldn't give greetings of any kind, and refused to give eye contact with anyone. She stayed in her room, and only answered direct questions from the boss. She was giving herself, and everyone around her, the silent treatment. She was absent every Thursday, taking her treatments. Her psychological defense was withdrawal.) Others have angry outbursts, becoming hostile, violent, and abusive. (One TV movie showed a man and a woman, who—upon dealing with their poor cancer prognoses—took their anger out on society, by using baseball bats to smash around 20 car windshields one night. Not productive, in the extreme.) Such responses cause further stress, and harmful side effects.

Many patients expect doctors to "fix them," without lifting a finger themselves, or changing their behavior even a tad, in order to help their own situation. They say they want to live, but don't act that way. For instance, a neighbor is a sweet freak, even though he has diabetes. He will eat a couple of doughnuts or a candy bar, and then jab himself in the stomach with an insulin shot. There are skin cancer patients who still bake in the sun. There are lung cancer patients who refuse to stop smoking. There are liver cancer patients who refuse to stop drinking alcohol. There are urology cancer patients who continue to deny the seriousness of their condition. Understand that those patients who do well make a concerted effort, and are motivated to improve their health situation. Your whole self (physical, mental, emotional, and spiritual) needs to be involved in your recovery.

The simple realization is that *you* are in control of your response to the cancer diagnosis, just as with the other ups and downs in your life (family, work, and community). Such an understanding is the foundation of stress management. Handling stress is all about taking charge of your thoughts, your emotions, and the way you deal with problems. Get rid of your excuses, and find ways to deal with your stress in positive ways.

Your positive ". . . thoughts of health and protection can heal," said Ernest Holmes. And thoughts of love, hope, happiness, pleasure, connection, creativity, and such, can also lead to self-healing. Such beliefs, alongside self-nurturing and self-pampering, can turn off the stress response, trigger the relaxation response, and return your body to its natural state.

Understand that worrying about your cancer now, and worrying about it recurring later, is common in survivors, because it feels completely out of your control. Realize that the more you talk about your worries, your troubles, and your fears, the more you breathe life into them. Consider that *all* situations have controllable and uncontrollable aspects. Deal with them without the drama.

You can feel in control through a positive frame of mind, and a proactive attitude: schedule and attend all your follow-up doctors' appointments; take any and all prescribed medications in an orderly fashion; take supplements, and use other coping skills, such as managing your anger, having a network of friends to talk with, exercise, rest, and so forth (while refraining from using tobacco, liquor, and/or overused, misused, or abused over-the-counter drugs).

You are advised to not waste one iota of time agitating about the fact that you are having worries, doubts, uncertainties, or confusion, as they are a part of every journey. Think of such negative thoughts as paper lions, tigers, and bears. Or, as Rev. Deborah L. Johnson suggests, see such thoughts as surrounded by a fog. "Don't fight the fog. You don't get mad at it, or go flailing around. You don't 'duke it out' with the fog." Simply know that the fog will lift. Or, see such thoughts as storm clouds, which come and go, and mean nothing. Dr. Gay Hendricks agrees, saying that: "Feelings are like rainstorms, because they have a beginning, a middle, and an end." Just notice them moving across your mind, and calmly turn them over to the Universe, to be quietly deactivated. You don't need to fuss and fret over them. Just say something like, "Oh, my. Here comes another doubt floating over," or "Another worry is passing through," and imagine it moving off. Let those random thoughts blow on by, as if pushed by a strong wind. Dr. Hendricks suggests that you identify with the sky, rather than the passing clouds that obscure it." Remember that the sun is always shining behind the clouds.

Think of such troubles as no more substantial than soap bubbles. Or a passing irritant, like indigestion. Consciously turn your efforts to something else. Stay positive, keep your focus on the healthy track, and keep on truckin'. Simply dwell on the end result—robust health—without fear, doubt, or worry.

May your troubles be less
And your blessings be more.
And nothing but happiness
Comes through your door.
—Irish Saying

ATTITUDE

Attitude is a little thing
that makes a big difference.
—Winston Churchill

Attitude is everything! You know that; you've heard it a hundred times. But in times of difficulties (such as hearing your cancer diagnosis), it may be challenging to maintain a positive mindset. Understand that your attitude toward cancer determines the intensity of your experience. Know that there is no faster way to bring about a worsening of your condition than to *think* it is coming. Your thought is a powerful force. Rather than worrying about your cancer, it would be a better use of your mental time to visualize a positive outcome. Bob Proctor says that, "You have the *choice* not to dwell on what-ifs."

As Ben Franklin said, "While we may not be able to control all that happens to us, we can control what happens inside of us." The right attitude, and the right mindset is all it takes. It's a choice. Stay clear of excessive dramatics. By remaining positive and calm, you place yourself in a more powerful position. "A positive attitude is the antidote to all suffering," says Dr. Wayne W. Dyer. True, your initial prognosis may be a shock. But you must find a way to improve the way you *feel* about it, right now, today, before things will start to get better for you. Gabor Maté, M.D., says that "Acceptance is simply the willingness to recognize and accept how things are." (*"I have the courage to continue."*)

Soften your attention to the cancer label, and begin to lean in the direction of this opportunity to get healthy. For your life to work, you need to be focusing forward, toward the future. Standing still, or constantly probing the past, isn't going to help your situation. Mike Dooley suggests: See your setbacks, delays, and detours, as simply steps in the mambo, tango, and cha-cha-cha. Don't stop dancing.

Dwell on what you can *do* about the situation. See beyond any self-defeating fears, doubts, and uncertainty, and begin looking for the good. Shift your vibration to the positive. When you think positive thoughts, you'll produce positive results. Studies show that having a cheerful attitude, and a fighting spirit, will improve your survival rate. Be happy. Take action! And expect things to work out. Healing begins in the mind. Barbara Morris, R.Ph., says, ". . . internalizing health consciousness is a preface to everything you do." Just get on with it.

It is written that Dr. Carl Jung—who founded analytical psychology—would tell his friends who reported a negative experience or tragic event, "Let us open a bottle of wine. Something good will come of this." In the same manner, priests, preachers, and rabbis, have been heard to say something on the order of: "Somehow this was meant to be. Look on the sunny side of the street. God is redirecting you. Something good will come of this."

Sure, there will be obstacles, dark days, growing pains, and knuckleheads that stand in your way, says Mike Dooley. That is a given, on your cancer journey. As such, he encourages you to face your next challenge and welcome it: "Rise up, don't back down. See it as a stepping-stone, not a wall; a valley, not an abyss." Refuse to give up. Understand that what you think, say, and do today influences your tomorrow.

Lisa Nichols (in *The Secret*), says that people tend to ". . . look at the things they don't want, and then give them just as much energy, if not more, with the idea that they can stamp it out; they can eliminate it, obliterate it. In our society, we've become content with fighting against cancer, fighting against poverty, fighting against war, fighting against drugs, fighting against terrorism, fighting against violence. We tend to fight everything we don't want, which actually creates more of a fight." As such, you are actually drawing more attention to the very experience that you are trying to avoid.

Or, as Rev. Deborah L. Johnson simply puts it: "You bring about what you think about. You want your circumstances to be better, so start putting your attention on betterment." There is no faster way to have a bad experience with cancer, than to think it is coming. There is no faster way to die of cancer than to think it is coming. Your constant worry and apprehension about cancer will ensure its arrival. Your thought is important. Your positive attitude is that powerful. Know that, as Abraham-Hicks explains, ". . . you get what you think about, whether you want it or not. And chronic thoughts about unwanted things invite, or ask for, matching experiences." That's what the Law of Attraction is all about. Choose to work toward health.

"Worry is often the cause of illness," says Dr. Masaru Emoto. It is detrimental to healing. Worrying is like pouring gasoline on a fire. Make your old habits of worry, doubt, and fear, a thing of the past. Become indifferent to them. "Just let them flow through your consciousness, acknowledge them, and return to your positive statements and images," advises Shakti Gawain. You can choose to sow thoughts of uncertainty, conflict, and depression, or you can choose to sow thoughts of health, self-empowerment, and a cancer-free existence.

As Todd Michael, M.D., D.O., FACOFP, says, "When things are good, say good things, and when things are bad, say twice as many good things." Drop all negative talk. No flip-flopping, no waffling, no wavering. Take corrective actions. Remain confident. Always keep your inner chatter positive. "When you have an attitude of positive thinking, your health improves," Dr. Emoto continues. Have a can-do attitude.

To paraphrase Neale Donald Walsch: Your enthusiasm means everything. Such enthusiasm (or lack thereof) will directly determine how successful any undertaking will be. So it behooves you to be excited about getting healthy and cancer-free, at the very core of your being, and to demonstrate that excitement in everything you think, say, and do.

Feeling excited about your well-being, and actively working towards your cancer-free goal, enhances both your health and happiness. Total engagement (physically, mentally, and emotionally) is crucial. A study by Jacquelyn B. James and colleagues, from the Sloan Center on Age and Work at Boston College (2012, cited by *Press-Telegram* columnist Helen Dennis), has found that "a half-hearted involvement is no better than no involvement at all," to which you could expect dismal results. So it would behoove you to go all-out in your endeavors.

Realize that your most difficult moments can bring you gifts. Life calls upon you to be philosophical at this pivotal time, and embrace the lows as well as the highs. Instead of feeling like a victim of a difficult cancer reality, become a catalyst for positive change. (*"I am my own cheering section!"*) Stand strong. Expect to feel good, and your positive attitude will help to create it, no matter your circumstances. What you believe comes to pass: a self-fulfilling prophecy. (*"I am generating health."*) Turn your stumbling blocks into stepping stones. Remember the words of Dr. William James: "The greatest discovery of my generation is that a human being can alter his life by altering his attitude of mind."

Refuse to say anything negative about yourself. The most important thing you can do is to *focus* on the positive. Focus on your whole health (not just cancer). Focus on a favorable outcome (not gloom and doom). Focus on your future (not your past or your present problems). Your quality of life depends upon your attitude toward your cancer. Neither loss nor adversity nor cancer should keep you from generating positive thoughts. Instead of being problem oriented, be solution oriented. Look for the positive. See the positive in all situations. Find something to be truly happy about, which will raise your vibrations. Believe Carlos Warter, M.D., Ph.D., when he says, "A positive, dedicated, life-affirming attitude is the key to the healing process."

Realize that you choose how you approach each day. Your attitude plays an enormous role in creating or destroying your health. Wake up with love in your heart, and a smile on your face. Start your day on the right foot. Pretend you are walking on sunshine, no matter the weather. Look on the bright side. Cherish everyone around you. See the value of your life. Understand that your healing requires a positive attitude, as well as dedication, and commitment.

Consider the words of Lewis L. Dunnington: "Your living is determined not so much by what life brings you, as by the attitude you bring to life; not so much by what happens to you, as by the way your mind looks at what happens." Recognize that you are free to choose your reactions and responses to life. Have you seen the 2015 Ford Edge TV commercial? A woman driver softly says: "Two million, 434 thousand, 311 people in this city, and only one me. I'll take those odds," as the 'Odds" song by Rachel Platten plays in the background. Now *that's* the right attitude!

Think healthful thoughts. Sandra Anne Taylor says that: "Your attitude is a primary catalyst both to what you magnetize and what you manifest." Actively participate. Do whatever it takes to become cancer-free and healthy again.

Lama Surya Das asks: "What shall I do with this precious life right now?" Consider further: What is your reason for overcoming cancer? What will you be doing?

What's next? The poet, Mary Oliver, also asks, "What is it you plan to do with your one wild and precious life?" How will you be spending time? With whom? What will you be studying? What goals will you be pursuing?

Note that anyone with a will to live can put up with almost any negative. You might want something more in your life. This cancer may be a call to new adventures, wider horizons, or an entirely different existence. Or maybe you just want a deeper meaning in your life, and to be fully engaged with whatever you are experiencing. Hold an attitude of positive expectancy. It all comes down to: What are you living for? Go all-out!

Our greatest freedom is
the freedom to choose our attitude.
—Viktor E. Frankl, M.D., Ph.D.

INTENTION

Every intention is
a trigger for transformation.
—Deepak Chopra, M.D.

Now that you have received the cancer news, there is much for you to process. There is much to think about, contemplate, evaluate, reconsider, reconstruct, realign, and transform. "Loss on any scale is a time to re-evaluate your priorities," L.D. Thompson tells us.

Intention is having a mighty purpose, a grand vision, accompanied by a determination to achieve that result: commitment. Intent is having a *Yes!* in your heart. Anyone who has been paying attention during the last several decades, realizes that physicists and metaphysicians have arrived at the same conclusion: *Form follows thought.* Intent is the mother of creation. Intention determines everything. As such, your focused thoughts have a powerful intention, a creative intent. "Your experience follows your intention," states

Doreen Virtue. And Dr. Wayne W. Dyer, in *The Power of Intention*, says, "Research suggests that intention on its own heals."

There are some who will say, "Face reality! The fact is, you have cancer." While experts say, what you focus on grows and expands. If you are constantly railing against what you consider to be the injustice of your cancer situation, you are not moving in the direction of growth and improvement. Adjust your focus (like a camera or telescope). Remember: Dr. Dyer says to "Shift from what you don't want, to what you do want." Don't focus on cancer. Concentrate on your well-being.

Obsessing about your cancer, thinking only of your cancer, keeps that image in front of you. Turn away from that condition. Cancel any thoughts of cancer. Neutralize negative thoughts. Instead, think of wellness. Look only at what you hope for: health. Place your thoughts on what you *want,* in order to attract something different. Look beyond the mud, the muck, and mire of what-is, to what you desire. Then turn those desires into intentions. If you zero in on cancer, you get more cancer. It you center your thoughts on health, you get more health. What you imagine in your mind becomes your world, Dr. Masaru Emoto tells us. "If you express your intentions, the realization of those intentions will follow." That's what the Law of Attraction is all about. Your thoughts are the forerunners of your experiences; your intentions are creating your future.

Turn your hazy thoughts and wishful, hopeful desires into potent intentions. Set your recovery goals, and work toward them, without wavering. The important thing is to shift from what you don't want, to what you *do* want. Keep your eye on the end result: healed and healthy. Be specific. Persistence counts. Determination counts. Hold a pit-bull, no-holds-barred attitude. Sandra Anne Taylor says that ". . . continued action greatly expands intention. The more you undertake, the more energy you send out regarding your intention." She further advises: "Intend the best and take positive action in every direction." Allow yourself to be healed.

"Intention is the mother of creation," declares Rev. Deborah L. Johnson. Your intention is key. Intend to be cured. Place all your focused energy on knowing—beyond a shadow of a doubt—that you can be healed, and *will* be healed. Such certainty enables you to relax, knowing health is on the way, regardless of how present circumstances may appear. Dr. Carlos Warter says that: "Intention and personal power are more potent than any manmade chemical."

Expect the best. Expectations influence results. When you set clear intentions, focusing on them with strong emotion, and take action, you are setting up a self-fulfilling prophecy. Your intention determines everything. Keep your eye on the prize, and keep the flame in your heart burning. Dr. Eldon Taylor, author of over 300 books, says, "The magic bullet for everything is spelled *intentional effort*." Join the strong and determined ones who have made the decision to live beyond their cancer prognosis. Become one with your intention. Feel inspired.

Life proceeds out of
your intention for it.
—Neale Donald Walsch

AFFIRMATIONS

An affirmation is a statement that is true
in the grand scheme of things,
but may not be an observable fact
in our lives right now.
—Victoria Moran

One way to be proactive is by using affirmations. To affirm is to state as a fact; to assert strongly; to make firm. Affirmations are positive statements that something is *already so* (achieved, attained, done, finished, accomplished). They are positive self-statements; conscious autosuggestions. They state a goal, a way you want to feel or be. Written, silently read, said aloud, or sung, this technique can produce extraordinary results. It is a great do-it-yourself tool. Affirmations can help change your belief system. You are reminding yourself, over and over again, of what you want to create; what you want to achieve. You are rewiring your thinking. As Muhammad Ali said, "I am the greatest! I said that even before I knew I was."

You are responsible for what you think. "Repeated or habitual thought creates what manifests around you," declares L.D. Thompson. "Through repetition, things are embedded into your subconscious," agrees David Cameron Gikandi. ". . . repeat, repeat, and repeat positive affirmations to yourself, every day, all day, and the subconscious will eventually believe." Adding, "Repetition causes internalization." And concluding, "Repetition is powerful." So steer your consistent thoughts toward what you want to create in your life: total and complete health.

Refuse to entertain negative thoughts. Self-edit your vocabulary, thoughts, and spoken words, so you no longer affirm cancer as your reality. Think instead of health and personal well-being. Remember, what you focus on enlarges. Fill your time with affirmations. They will inspire you to a better-feeling state, and project into the future what you want to experience: a cancer-free healthy body.

The constant repetition of positive affirmations help to keep you focused on your goal. "They do not deny the reality of your situation, but provide something stronger and more powerful than your worries and concerns to think about," says Father Paul Keenan, in his book, *Good News for Bad Days*. They are retraining your thinking, through your very own commercials.

You are consciously, and emphatically, attempting to better yourself. Affirmations keep you on track. They counteract any negative self-talk, or self-sabotaging behaviors. *("I deserve the best.")*

Be bold. Affirm it. Declare it to be a fact, and always in the present tense. It often includes the words *I am*. ("*I am strong. I am fit. I am healthy.*") Say what you want, not what you don't want. ("*My body is healing! I am healing. I am healing now.*") Say your affirmation into your mirror, or shout it aloud in your car. Sandra Anne Taylor says that when you say affirmations out loud, ". . . your acoustic energy amplifies your electromagnetic vibrations and doubles their power." Louise L. Hay agrees, saying: "The most powerful way to do affirmations is to look in a mirror and say them aloud." Or you can mentally repeat them at random moments, while standing in line at the bank, post office, or grocery store. Say affirmations while doing any mundane task (washing dishes, vacuuming, taking a bath or showering, washing your car, or watering the lawn). Replay affirmations, poems, or prayers in your mind, as you walk anywhere. Fill your wasted time with them.

Dr. Art Martin suggests that you write your affirmations 21 times a day, for 21 days, whereas other experts suggest that you say your affirmation throughout the day—even hundreds of times, in the very beginning—to lock in the new programming. Others say morning, noon, and night, are enough. Bernie Siegel, M.D. maintains that,

"By repeating an affirmation over and over again, it becomes embedded in the subconscious, and eventually it becomes your reality." *("I am surging with high-octane energy and glowing health.")*

"As a rule of thumb, the less cluttered the affirmation, the clearer the effect," says Gregg Braden. And Shakti Gawain agrees: ". . . the shorter and simpler the affirmation, the more effective." Use 3x5 cards, on which to write your own affirmations. Start with one short statement, adding other longer sentences later. (I carry a stack in my purse, and have another 100 cards—with written affirmations on both the front and back—in the house.) Use colored ink to emphasize or underscore certain words. Stick Post-it notes in specific sites around your rooms (such as on your nightstand to view as you first get up in the morning, and the last thing you see before you go to sleep at night), or by your landline phones, and in your car, or on your calendar and computer. Place them in your wallet or pockets. Leave them in unusual places (medicine cabinet, drawers, as bookmarks) to surprise yourself. Surround yourself with positive self-talk. (*"I think in healthy ways. I act in healthy ways. I am healthy in all ways."*) You can even record your personal affirmations, to listen to while walking, jogging, bicycling, or driving, to keep your attention on your wellness goals.

And let's not forget, Émile Coué (1857-1926), the French psychologist and pharmacist, who became famous for encouraging people to look into their mirrors, and repeat, *"Every day in every way, I am getting better and better."* You can add a slight change, to say: *"Every day in every way, my health is getting better and better."* Say such affirmations with confidence, and *believe* them.

I also have a growing collection of ampersands (**&**), made out of wood, metal, plastic, and fabric, along with a couple of paintings. Some are small, others are average-sized and large, while a few are HUGE, that are scattered throughout my house. To me, they are a physical trigger for an affirmation. Whenever my eyes see one, my mind automatically thinks: *"**And** the best is yet to come."*

Use your inner speech to stay focused on your intentions. Carolyn Scott Kortge says, "Affirmations, mantras, poems, and prayers become internal 'therapists' redirecting the focus to thoughts that provide inspiration and reassurance." Repeat your own affirmations throughout each day (such as: *"Wellness is my natural state," "I am healthy, strong, and able,"* and *"I am in excellent shape"*). Saturate your mind with what you want to be true for you (*"I am happy. I am healthy. I am healed!"*).

That is your goal,
that the affirmations you create
become hard-wired into your system.
—Dr. Eric Maisel

MANTRAS

The mantra becomes one's staff of life
and carries one through every ordeal.
—Mahatma Gandhi

While you're at it, you might consider mantras, which is another form of autosuggestion. A mantra can be a sound, a syllable, a single word, or a short group of words that are considered capable of creating a transformation. Mantras are words that provide mental focus, and keep your mind in the present moment, blocking out distracting or negative thoughts.

"Emotions are where it's at, and creating a mantra will help you feel them," says Mike Dooley. If your mind is going around in circles, and you can't stop thinking unwanted the-sky-is-falling thoughts, mantras help you to calm down, by repeating a word or a phrase to yourself. Dharma Khalsa, M.D., says they "turn off your worries and reduce your stress, simply because your mind is preoccupied with your mantra." Mantras are also used in walking meditation.

Neale Donald Walsch tells us, ". . . if you repeat a thought, or say a word, over and over again—not once, not twice, but dozens, hundreds, thousands of times—do you have any idea of the creative power of that?" He continues on, "A thought or a word expressed and expressed and expressed becomes just that—expressed. That is, pushed out. It becomes outwardly realized. It becomes a physical reality."

Gregg Braden's book, *The Isaiah Effect*, tells of a film that shows a woman with a cancerous tumor—three inches in diameter—in a hospital bed. Three men stood behind the patient, and in unison, participated in a centuries old mode of healing: chanting. "They repeated a single word over and over again, a word that became louder and more intense as the healing progressed. Loosely translated into English, they were saying, "already gone," or "already accomplished." In two minutes and 40 seconds, the tumor disappeared. It is said that the key was on *the feeling of the outcome*. The doctors were astounded at what they had witnessed.

You can use mantras to attract what you want into your life. For example: When I ingest my meds and vitamins, I mentally chant: *Transform, regenerate, renew.* When my brother, Terry L. Neal, takes his daily walks, he chants, *Wisdom, health, wealth and happiness.* Louise L. Hay suggests that you repeat, *All is well.* Many are those who chant, *Peace, peace, peace*, or *Joy, joy, joy*. Dr. Wayne Dyer suggests that you make *yes* your inner mantra, or shout *Yes!* aloud. Try, *Perfect health*, or *Health, health, health*, or the old standby, *Healthy, wealthy, and wise*.

Using a mantra, is also the perfect time to show how grateful you are for each day. The silent repetition of a single message (Thank you, Gracias, Merci, Danke schoen) in whatever language you choose, simply focuses on what you already have in your life, and appreciating it. You needn't be specific about any one thing you are grateful for—your doctor, your family, your friends, your support group, your general health, working toward a wellness goal—just lump them altogether in your mind, with a general thank you to the Universe, showing your gratitude. *Thank you, thank you, Thank you. . .*

If we chant while
simultaneously holding an idea,
the mental picture manifests
the physical form rapidly.
—Doreen Virtue

VISUALIZATIONS

Everyone visualizes.
Losers visualize the penalties of failure.
Winners visualize the rewards of success.
—Dr. Rob Gilbert

To visualize merely means to picture something, to form an image, or paint a portrait in your mind. They are visual affirmations. You simply focus on that photo or movie in your brain. You mentally see what you want, exactly as you want it to be, as if it were physically present. Use your imagination, and picture yourself cancer-free, and enjoying yourself. Take time each day for a mental rehearsal (like a purposeful daydream) or some guided imagery practice. Allow your mind to influence the health and well-being of your body. Mentally see yourself doing what you want, while feeling healthy, and looking great. See an endless stream of green lights in your life.

Consider the words of Dr. William James: "There is a law in psychology that if you form a picture in your mind of what you would like to be, and you keep and hold that picture long enough, you will soon become exactly as you have been thinking." Again, focus on what you want; the outcome or solution.

Dr. Jean Achterberg used a healing imagery approach to health. One popular example is that in which the patient would visualize the bad cancer cells being consumed by the good white blood cells.

However, other experts suggest that you don't visualize what is happening with your cancer, or any unwanted experience, or sense of lack. Move your attention away from unpleasant situations. Constantly imagining, picturing what you want—the end result—will help you manifest it in your life. Simply see yourself as beautiful, free of pain, and sound in body, mind, and spirit. Visualize your wonderful, healthy body, and appreciate its strength and flexibility. See it in joyful circumstances, doing what you most like to do. Picture your whole body as happy, and humming with light. Take that mental snapshot, and return to it anytime. Constancy matters.

Visualizing the end result of your cancer treatment helps you to achieve a subconscious blueprint for your future. Sandra Anne Taylor suggests that you "Visualize your problem lifting up and floating away like a cloud on the horizon." Shift from a linear mindset to a cyclical mindset, joining the beginning of your cancer treatments with the end ("alpha and omega thinking," according to Dr. Wayne W. Dyer), via visualization. Consciously cultivate a clear mental picture of your body being cancer-free, via the successful completion of your treatment. *See* yourself healthy, filled with vim, vigor, and vitality.

Dr. Dyer speaks from experience. After reading Dr. Maxwell Maltz's *Psycho-Cybernetics*, while in Guam in 1961 (about healing with the power of the mind), he refused surgery, and chose self-healing through visualization. His cyst completely disappeared, and he had no further need for medical treatment. Fifty years later, he was diagnosed with leukemia, and continually visualized his healthy body, with the same outstanding results. Now, he's happy that he had that first cyst experience, saying that ". . . everything that shows up in our lives, does so for a reason."

"Your mind's images are literally the blueprint from which your world is built," says David Cameron Gikandi. Revisit this snapshot on a daily basis. This is not a hit or miss proposition. Bob Proctor says, "You must be personally involved with making it happen on a daily basis." Get in the habit of beginning each morning, visualizing your cancer-free body. See yourself surrounded by a Healing Bubble. Before you get out of bed, begin visualizing your day, as successful sports professionals, business executives, celebrities, and politicians do, on a daily basis

(Oprah Winfrey, Jim Carrey, Tiger Woods, and Arnold Schwarzenegger, to name a few).

"Visualize, it's the least you can do," says Mike Dooley, who maintains that once each morning, for five minutes, is sufficient. Or at anytime during your day. Or just before you fall asleep at night. That's it! *How easy can anything get?* You are simply seeing the end result you want. And Shakti Gawain adds, "Five minutes of conscious positive visualization can balance out hours, days, even years of negative patterns."

Consider Ludwig Van Beethoven: By 1818 he was 48 years old, and stone-cold deaf. Five years later, he finished his extraordinary Ninth Symphony! He never heard it. He just *imagined* it! And we all have the same ability to form images, to think new ideas, to fantasize, to dream up . . . Remember the words of Albert Einstein: "Imagination is more important than knowledge. Knowledge is limited. Imagination circles the world."

Neale Donald Walsch says, "Imagination is your greatest gift. Imagine yourself as okay right now. Totally okay. Imagine yourself as Whole, Complete, and Perfect. With nothing to change, nothing to 'improve.' See it in your mind's eye." He then continues: "Can you imagine this? Then you have just created Tomorrow."

Imagine your cancer-free body. See that your tumor cells are powerless against your own body's natural healing resources. Vividly focus on the details of the scene (sights, sounds, colors, textures, people). *Feel* your emotions, as if it were happening now. Dwell only on the end result. Simply close your eyes for a short time each day, and visualize your body being healthy and cancer-free.

"If doubts or contradictory thoughts arise," suggests Shakti Gawain in her book, *Creative Visualization*, "don't resist them or try to prevent them. This will tend to give them a power they don't otherwise have. Just let them flow through your consciousness, acknowledge them, and return to your positive statements and images."

Positive visualization lifts your consciousness from thoughts of fear and failure to happiness and success. Never spend any time agitating over *how* it's going to happen. Let go of the hows. "Pitch the logic. And drop the 'cursed hows,'" says Mike Dooley. Dwell only on the end goal, where you have already arrived, safe and sound!

Even Richard Bach, in his hugely popular 1970s best seller, *Jonathan Livingston Seagull*, has his bird character thinking and visualizing from his desired end result:

Chiang spoke slowly and watched the
younger gull ever so carefully.
"To fly as fast as thought, to anywhere," he said,
"you must begin by knowing that
you have already arrived."

The trick is to not only imagine your body as totally healthy, but *feeling* the emotions involved at the same time. Understand that an emotional state affects the chemical makeup of your body. Choose which emotions you engage. (*"I happily spread joy wherever I go."*) Shakti Gawain explains that, "The clearer and stronger your intention, the more quickly and easily your creative visualization will work."

Note, however, that in order for a lasting manifestation, you must work in tandem, making changes in yourself. You need to make every effort to work towards wellness, while, at the same time, visualizing your end result of total health.

Dr. Eldon Taylor speaks highly about the positive aspects of the envisioning process, suggesting that you energize your efforts in every way, through visualization: "The visualization process is a magnet of sorts, and whether it's the observer interacting with the observed, a function of physics, or a matter of self-fulfilling prophecy, the difference is truly academic." And Sandra Anne Taylor sums it up by saying, "Imagery is everything."

Creative visualization sets you up to win, says Alan Cohen. In your imagination, see yourself deliriously jumping up and down, whooping with joy. You can even throw in a ticker-tape parade, while confetti swirls around, as you dance about, turning somersaults and backflips—with pyrotechnics exploding in the background. Seeing is believing. *Believe* that this final healthy state has already come to pass. Produce what you want to happen. Set the stage for your cancer-free event.

Visualization techniques can greatly improve the effectiveness of conventional medical treatment.
—Emmett E. Miller, M.D.

EXERCISE/MOVEMENT

Those who think
they have no time for bodily exercise
will sooner or later
have to find time for illness.
—Edward Stanley

Christine Northrup, M.D., concurs, saying: "On average, regular exercise adds seven healthy years to your life. So when someone tells me she doesn't have time to exercise, I always reply that being dead seven years prematurely really eats up a lot of time too." Wow! That sure puts it in perspective. And, she cites an eight-year study that showed ". . . as little as an hour *a week* of moderate exercise can cut your risk of developing chronic disease sevenfold." Who knew?

One of the crucial needs of your body is simply to move. As such, there is nothing that is more consistently prescribed by doctors than to exercise regularly. It is the best-known, scientifically-proven method to significantly reduce stress, and release the chronic tension in your life.

Actually, any kind of activity that gets you *moving* is good for you: dancing, Tai Chi, aerobics, martial arts, bicycling, skating, sports, and so on. You needn't invest in a gym membership or expensive equipment. Realize that exercise, laughter, and play are closely related. Give fun a high priority in your life. In addition, Robert Arnot, M.D., says, "Exercise is the magic bullet for creating mental energy, and the feeling of optimism." Not only that, but Gary Small, M.D. reports on recent studies indicating that physical exercise also improves memory function.

Andrew Weil, M.D., recommends that people make walking their primary form of exercise, calling it the overall best exercise. Many experts—in various fields—suggest walking for health. They recommend walking for a minimum of 20 minutes, three times a week, or ten minutes each day. It is said that you think better on your feet, and exercise feeds your brain, as in fresh air equals fresh attitudes. "A vigorous walk will do more good for an unhappy, but otherwise healthy adult, than all the medicine and psychology in the world," said Paul Dudley White, M.D. And Dr. Wayne W. Dyer suggests that when you go for a walk alone, you can enhance the experience by repeating a mantra in time to your footsteps—a phrase or a single word, such as love, beauty, or health. Walkers are known to be people who step out with purpose, step forward, and make a move. View daily walks as a good investment in your health and well-being.

Exercise is a good prescription for cancer patients. Dan Millman suggests that you start with one jumping jack a day, or a mere three minutes a day. "In a year, those three little minutes have become more than sixty hours." Keep moving. Get out of your chair, and move around. Get off of that couch, and move around. Christiane Northrup, M.D. says research shows that nonstop sitting increases your risk of cancer, as well as your risk of dying in the next three years, by 40 percent! Cancer research supports the idea that those with such a diagnosis should be active throughout all stages of their survivorship, to improve their quality of life, as well as long-term outcomes. The benefits include:

*Reducing fatigue;
*Improving balance and flexibility;
*Boosting energy and mood;
*Improving heart and bone health; and,
*Cutting your risk of cancer returning.

You are advised to start slowly, with only moderate physical activity. Move forward at your own pace, knowing that progress builds steadily. Even small changes can make a difference. Engage in things that are fun, that make you laugh.

Physical exercise appears
not only to keep brain cells alive,
but also to grow new neurons.
—Gary Small, M.D.

REST/RELAXATION

For fast-acting relief, try slowing down.
—Lily Tomlin

Do you remember Simon & Garfunkel's "59th Street Bridge" song lyrics? "Slow down, you move too fast," are wise words from 1966. "Cancer is telling you to slow down," says Lissa Rankin, M.D. "Listen to your body." Experts agree: You need to unplug, let go, unwind, put your feet up, and relax. Revive the lost art of hanging out, with no agenda, and no destination. Do some puttering. Take periodic time-outs: Pace yourself: pause, do, pause, do, pause, do. You need to factor in some downtime, and refrain from cancer worries. Mellow out. Savor your life. Give your overworked brain and body a rest. Relaxation is essential to ensure your health and well-being. Dr. Rankin further says that "Only in this rested, relaxed state can your body repair itself."

As Ashleigh Brilliant says, "Sometimes the most urgent and vital thing you can possibly do is take a complete rest." Move from the fast lane, to a slower lane of existence. "Perhaps the best thing you can do right now is *nothing at all*," advises Neale Donald Walsch.

In an attempt at full transparency, let me just say that I found this extremely difficult to do. I had always been a whirling dervish, having on all occasions a number of projects going at the same time, while traveling here, there, and everywhere. My comfort zone was chaos, and stress was my middle name. Happily, my life is no longer like a continual air raid drill: *Incoming!* I have traded in an avalanche of activity and accomplishment, in order to ease up, refresh myself, and recover my strength. I am learning to relax. After a long time of adjustment, I found to my utter shock and dismay, that I actually like it! Only in a rested, relaxed state can your body repair itself. Relaxation frees the body to do what it does naturally—heal itself.

Allowing stress to affect you can lead to depression, and you can't afford that extra strain. Get your anxiety under control by relaxing. "Relaxation therapies may help to alleviate certain symptoms of cancer, relieve treatment side effects, and improve your sense of well-being," explains Sheryl M. Ness, RN. Engage your mind (through words, music, and images) to help your healing, via the use of Guided

Imagery or Meditation CDs (such as the "Pre-Surgical Guided Imagery Program" by Blue Shield, featuring psychotherapist, Belleruth Naparstek, LISW, BCD.). Understand that the state of relaxation frees your body to repair itself, increasing your comfort and speed of recovery. Keeping your noise level down gives you time for reflection and reevaluation.

Take periodic time-outs during your day. Downtime allows you to recuperate, reenergize, and recharge your life. Experts suggest that you calm down and lounge around; relax with a good book, unwind with a hobby, or snuggle with your pet. Have plenty of interludes in which you do nothing but putter about, wander around, and be totally unproductive. Don't plan on the when and how of your leisure time, just do what comes to mind, when it comes to mind. Your body knows when it needs to take a break. Massage, meditation, yoga, listening to soft music or the soothing sounds of nature, or simply singing in the shower, can place you in a state of relaxation.

"Anything not worth doing is worth not doing well. Think about it," said Eli Angel, quoted by Robert Fulghum. Even just *imagining* resting (at the beach, or in the woods, or on a mountain top), can do the trick. Know, too, that a loving thought can relax your entire body. Any conscious effort you make to relax, both mentally or physically, will reduce your stress. *("I can release and let go.")*

Rest is not idleness,
and to lie sometimes on the grass
under the trees on a summer's day,
listening to the murmur of water
and watching the clouds float across the sky,
is by no means a waste of time."
—John Lubbock

SLEEP/NAPS

Everything you do,
you'll do better,
with a good night's sleep.
—Dr. Michael Breus

"Restful sleep accelerates healing, and enlivens renewal," Deepak Chopra, M.D., the author of more than eighty books, tells us. All doctors tell us that we need six to eight hours of restful sleep each night, without the aid of sleeping pills. (And that's normal, without chemotherapy, radiation, or surgery.) Sleep difficulties visit 75 percent of us at least a few nights per week (reports the Harvard Women's Health Watch), while another study places the findings higher, in the 90-plus percent range.

Michael F. Roizen, M.D., chief wellness officer of the Cleveland Clinic, states, "Sleep is the most underrated health habit." David M. Rapoport, M.D., director of the NYU Sleep Disorders Program, agrees, saying,

"Sleep used to be kind of ignored, like parking our car in a garage and picking it up in the morning." Not anymore. Humans *need* sleep, along with food, water, and oxygen, to survive. "Sleep is an integral part of all health, particularly brain health," states Dr. Joseph Mercola. And Arianna Huffington presents cutting-edge scientific studies that speak to the indisputable benefit of sleep, in her 14th book, *Thrive*.

Not only does adequate sleep make you feel better, boosting your mood, and alleviating under-eye circles, but it benefits your over-all health (heart, weight, blood pressure, immune system, and mind). Studies have shown that if you wake up at three in the morning, and can't get back to sleep, your immune cells can't work as well for the next 24 hours. (Bad news for me!)

"Poor sleep increases your likelihood of getting cancer," Dr. Mercola states. And a study (discussed in a *Brain, Behavior, and Immunity* 2003, October issue) showed that how well you sleep may determine how well your body can fight cancer: sleep problems alter the balance of cortisol and melatonin, which can cause a more rapid progression of cancer.

On the flip side, Chellie Campbell has another suggestion: Upon waking up in the middle of the night, remind yourself that no matter how much or how little sleep you got that night, that it would be enough. And that you would feel rested, alert, and full of energy in the morning. She says that sometimes she gets eight hours of sleep and feels great, and sometimes she gets only four hours of sleep—and she still feels great. Use positive affirmations. *("I get all the sleep I need each night, and I awake refreshed and energized each morning!")*

And while you're at it, "Attend to your dreams. Give yourself a chance to learn from them," Judith Orloff, M.D., advises. (At length, I finally paid attention to my dreams, and what they were trying to tell me. As such, I dodged a bullet, and *lived,* as a result. But that is a different story, for another time, as told in *The Bogeyman: Stalking and its Aftermath*). Dreams are important. Don't dismiss them. Dreams are an inner guide.

Throughout history and all around the world, ancient kings had dream interpreters, and shamans, the Senoi tribe in Malaysia, Aboriginals, native tribes, and dream researchers, all remind us that dreams are an important part of our lives. To which Sigmund Freud, M.D. (a neurologist and the father of psychoanalysis) agreed, famously saying that, ". . . the dream is the royal road to the unconscious." Carl G. Jung, M.D., Ph.D. (a psychiatrist, a psychotherapist, and the father of analytical psychology), also believed that dreams were messages from the soul, and could be premonitions, warning people of dangers and impending disasters, and even death.

Although you spend a third of your life sleeping, you only dream approximately two hours each night: four or five dreams a night, spending about 20 percent of your total sleep in the dream state. So, during a typical lifespan, when you turn 70, you will have spent six years of your life in the dream world. Experts suggest that you dream more than one thousand dreams a year, whether or not you remember them. Dreams are meaningful. Pay attention to your dreams, and respect them.

Immerse yourself in the subject of dreams. (I own 62 books on the subject alone, and tons more with chapters on dreams.) Understand that you are an original; no one else is exactly, precisely, like you. You are one of a kind. As a result, your dreams will not be the same as anyone else's. So you are the best interpreter. What is the meaning of each of your dreams? What is their collective message? Know that dreams are not meant to conceal, but to reveal, as your inner self is talking to you. Important dream messages will be repeated, in varying ways, until you get the idea. (I finally came to see that a whole number of my dreams were saying the same thing, in different ways. Yikes!)

Honor your dreams by paying attention, and gaining deeper insights into your fears, needs, and truths. Calvin S. Hall, Jr., Ph.D., a psychologist and dream research pioneer, is credited with saying, "A dream is like a personal document, a letter to oneself." So take a tip from an old Yiddish proverb: "A dream which has not been interpreted is like a letter unread."

Dr. Mercola suggests that you eat the following foods several times a week, to promote sleep: almonds, walnuts, avocados, Chamomile tea, cherries, and green leafy vegetables. Many suggest taking a melatonin supplement, to help you fall asleep faster, and stay asleep. (Melatonin is also said to have anticancer properties.)

Fatigue, tiredness, and naps go hand-in-hand. Take naps: Morning, afternoon, or both, who cares? Your body needs the sleep. It is a fact that survivors rest. Even short naps help. As a cancer patient, you can't—and aren't—expected to continue at the same pace as before your treatments or surgery. In fact, the big problem for cancer patients is that they take too much on themselves, keeping up their same stressful schedules, which hinders their bodies' ability to cope with their illness.

It is essential to take catnaps (a short doze while sitting up), longer naps, or a deep, long sleep whenever needed. This is not the time to feel indolent, slothful, and guilty about snoozing. After all, if famous nappers with such diverse backgrounds, talents, and careers, such as Aristotle, Albert Einstein, Leonardo Da Vinci, Salvador Dali, Johannes Brahms, Ludwig Van Beethoven, Ben Franklin, Thomas Edison, Napoleon, Winston Churchill, John D. Rockefeller, and former Presidents John F.

Kennedy, Lyndon B. Johnson, Ronald Reagan, and Bill Clinton, alongside that of Yogi Berra, Morgan Freeman, Magaret Thatcher, and Eleanor Roosevelt, took daily naps, why can't you? Naps are nothing to be ashamed of. After all, Henry Ford was heard to say: "I never stand up when I can sit down, and I never sit, when I can lie down."

Your body needs sleep and rest to repair, recover, and heal. "You're not healthy, unless your sleep is healthy," William Dement, M.D. says. And Robert Fulghum's Kindergarten Credo includes: "Take a nap every afternoon." He also suggests, "When in doubt, take a nap." As such, A.A. Milne (1882-1956), had the right idea, when he created the Winnie The Pooh character, who encouraged:

Let's begin by taking
a smallish nap or two. . .
—Winnie The Pooh

NUTRITION

Let food be thy medicine
and medicine be thy food.
-Hippocrates

Good nutrition is a core requirement for cancer patients. It must be taken seriously. "Health is a matter of choice, not a mystery of chance," says Robert A. Mendelssohn, M.D. Nutrition is the process of providing the food substances necessary for growth, repair, and maintenance of the body. Russell Blaylock, M.D., agrees, ". . . a combination of nutrients has a far better chance of controlling cancer than anything conventional medicine has to offer." So, through nutritional support, you can reduce the risk of getting cancer, or having a recurrence. And nutritional support, while undergoing chemotherapy and radiation, can dramatically increase your survival prospects. It is said that with good nutrition, a tumor will become benign in behavior.

Dharma Singh Khalsa, M.D., states that if you eat a diet that is composed mostly of grains, vegetables, and fruits, you'll not only be helping your brain, and heart, but you will also cut your cancer risk by *at least* half. (I wish I had known this earlier.) Deepak Chopra, M.D., adds that eating a variety of well-balanced foods, eating in moderation, and drinking pure water, is key. (*"I like vegetables, I like fruit, and I like water." "I eat vegetables, I eat fruit, and I drink water."*) For healthy living, all modern doctors still advise the same thing that Hippcrates—the Father of Medicine—said over 2,000 years ago: a proper diet, exercise, and fresh air.

Paul White, M.D., explains that: "Most health problems begin in the kitchen. Food preparation can make a critical difference in overcoming cancer. We are told to eat low-fat and nutrient-dense food, and make every bite count. Or, as many a mother has advised: Eat your vegetables, don't skip breakfast, don't live on sweets, and don't eat like a pig. All the things that doctors whole-heartedly recommend. Greg Anderson suggests that you eat actual food—"that means quality, real natural food." He says, "If it is boxed or bottled or canned or packaged, be skeptical." (When I was in another state, my son called me in a panic, "Mom! Hurry home! Dad is buying *bogus* cheese!" My husband hadn't heard about synthetic cheese.)

Many doctors maintain that cancer is fueled by eating fast foods, chemical additives, sugar, and artificial sweeteners. Yet know, as Robert A. Nagourney, M.D., points out, that the most mundane of foodstuffs—mustard, pickle relish, and ketchup—are of medicinal value. And, in his book *Outliving Cancer,* the whole chapter 13 shows the bona fide health *benefits* of garlic, red wine, and dark chocolate, in the role of cancer. So don't throw the baby out with the bathwater.

Barbara Morris, R.Ph., too, reminds us of our "food abuse" (grease, fried anything, refined sugar, processed foods, empty calories, and non-nutritious drinks and snacks). She further notes that not only do we eat socially, but we do so when we take breaks from almost anything, as well as when we watch movies and television. We eat for emotional comfort, and to assuage anger, relieve boredom, or depression.

"Eating patterns are directly connected with emotional issues, arising both from childhood and from current stresses," Gabor Maté, M.D. states. Be aware that stress often triggers impulse eating. (I am a sort-of recovering sugar addict—a sweet freak—and I can tell you that in moments of elevated stress, my unconscious sugar cravings would emerge with a vengeance. And I often found myself zooming headlong across town to the doughnut shop. Doughnuts and I have had a long-lasting affair for decades.) Are you aware that the average American eats 152 pounds of sugar each year? Not only that, but did you know that the average person in the U.S. drinks 57 gallons of soda each year?

(Sugar is considered to be cancer fuel! Who knew?) Egads!

Dr. Candace B. Pert, in her book, *Molecules of Emotion*, considers sugar to be a drug. She maintains that relying on sugar to give you a quick pick-me-up is as analogous to, if not as dangerous as, shooting heroin. Yikes! And Dr. Doreen Virtue explains that each food we crave corresponds with a specific feeling we want to soothe or mask with food. Both Deepak Chopra, M.D., and David Simon, M.D., suggest further sound advice: "Use food to feed your body, not your emotions."

Food can heal and renew.
—Deepak Chopra, M.D.

WATER

Water is the first principle of all things.
—Thales

"From a physical perspective, humans are water," Dr. Masaru Emoto tells us, in *The Hidden Messages of Water.* "We start out life being 99 percent water, as fetuses. When we are born, we are 90 percent water, and by the time we reach adulthood we are down to 70 percent. If we die of old age, we will probably be about 50 percent water. In other words, throughout our lives *we exist mostly as water.*" Water changes you from the inside out. You are essentially water.

In his fascinating research, Dr. Emoto has discovered that the molecules of water are affected by our thoughts, words, and feelings, as well as classical and uplifting music. His astounding photographs illustrate the beautiful, well-formed crystals of positive words and phrases, such as "Love," "Beauty," "Wisdom," "Gratitude," and "Let's do it!" Negative words and expressions ("Fool," "Kill," "You make me sick!") have the opposite affect, showing their power to deform and destroy.

Know that your words and intentions have an enormous impact upon your body, and the vibrations of your words have an affect on others around you. Saying unkind words causes damage to others, as well as water. Written words have the same affect. They actually emit a unique vibration that water senses. (Printing words on your water glass or jar, or even using stickers or adding pictures will work just as well). As such, it doesn't matter what language is being used, it's the vibration that counts. Use positive healing words.

Water has healing capabilities. It is circulated by blood and bodily fluids throughout your body, and serves as a transporter of energy. When you send positive thoughts and gratitude to the water you drink, its quality improves, and your health improves, as well. Understand that water is sensitive, and responds to what we say. It changes dramatically according to the information exposed to it.

Experts maintain that 70 percent of Americans aren't drinking enough water. (I, for instance, *never* drank water. Ever. My father was concerned about fluoride, chlorine, and heavy metals in tap water, so we only drank milk when I was growing up. I didn't like the taste of water, anyway. At all. It tasted like medicine, to me. (Translation: It wasn't sweet.) Finally, at 74 years of age, I was determined to take better care of my body. And I began drinking water: a sip at a time. It was slow going, at first, but I persevered. Now I can drink water without gagging! And I am very proud of achieving this milestone, for health reasons. (Which, of course, disproves the old adage that: "You can't teach old dogs new tricks"!) It is common knowledge that you can go without food for several days, but if you go without water, you'll die within a few days. You must be well hydrated to be healthy. It is vital in terms of energy production, and keeping the lymphatic system clean.

Water obtained from natural springs, glaciers, underground rivers, and the upper reaches of rivers, are best, experts tell us. They differ, however, on whether to drink bottled water, purified water, filtered water, mineral water, or boiled water, but they all agree on the primary need to drink five to eight glasses of water per day. But, "What kind of water will you have?" is a question few California restaurant servers and party hostesses ask anymore, due to our long-lasting drought. More people are drinking water now, due to its medicinal quality, while less water is available. (As a high school youngster, lo these many years ago, I was very concerned about future water wars and food wars, but I was hoping to have passed over by then. Not so. They are already upon us.)

Drinking tap water is not advised, as it doesn't form crystals, due to the addition of fluoride and chlorine in public water supplies. Tap water is linked to cancer, which has become the number one cause of death in Japan since 1981. Typical problems of old age—memory loss, confusion, and severe dementia—are now being linked to the *quality* of water, according to Dr. Emoto.

Your body naturally loses water every day, as it flushes out toxins, viruses, and bacteria, through elimination, perspiration, and even breathing. So water must continually be replaced for you to be optimally well. Sodas, diet sodas, sports drinks, coffee, milk, juices, and alcoholic beverages *do not count*. Although Andrew Weil, M.D., adds that you can augment hydration with drinks that are mostly water (tea, very diluted fruit juice, or sparkling water with lemon). Pure water should be your drink of choice. There is a correlation between drinking more water and having better health: You will look better and feel better.

The essence of a human being is water,
our lives begin with water and end with water.
—Dr. Masaru Emoto

SUPPLEMENTS

Most chemotherapy is designed to kill cancer cells,
while most supplements are designed to
strengthen the immune system
so that it can then remove cancer cells.
—Dr. Kelly A. Turner

Supplements are a cornerstone of healing and repair. Many people think that supplements are the missing link in their cancer healing. Most supplements have multiple uses and multiple benefits. Supplements are a must in today's toxic-soup world. Most supplements—vitamins, minerals, herbals, extracts, juices—are meant to create an internal environment that is so healthy, so vital and strong, that cancer cells are unable to flourish. Supplements are used to help a sick body regain balance and health. It is believed that supplements can take you to a higher level of well-being than is achievable by food alone. They make up for the vitamins and minerals that are lacking in today's food supply, due to depleted soils, industrial farming, hybridization techniques, and processed factory-made foods, as well as environmental toxins, and unhealthy choices.

"Vitamin deficiencies, even if very small, can have a significant effect on the health and well-being of your entire body," say Anne and David Frahm. And, "Taking your vitamins fills your body with what is needed to repair itself," says Lissa Rankin, M.D. Supplements also provide support for poor diet and lifestyle issues (while you address the issues of eating processed foods, drinking beer, smoking, and getting no exercise).

Joan Amtoft-Neilsen, M.D., Ph.D., D.C., suggests along with your cancer medications, that you add supplements, including vitamins, minerals, homeopathics, herbs, amino acids, and immune stimulants. She cautions you to use a product line that is known for its purity. She also suggests pure water.

Mark Hyman, M.D., also suggests, in *The Blood Sugar Solution*, that you think of supplements as a part of your diet, and become a smart supplement shopper. "You want the best-quality food and the best-quality supplements you can buy."

Taking supplements does not excuse you from eating a healthy diet, but if you are under stress—and most people with cancer are—you need additional nutrients, just as athletes do. Vitamin C, in particular, is burned up by stress. (I take 1,000 mg of vitamin C, three times a day.) Supplements help you to attain a higher degree of wellness. Granted, I don't have my nutrition act together, but I always take my vitamins and minerals with my orange juice, almonds or walnuts, to counteract said behavior. I take the old standby vitamins ABCE, as well as D-3 (considered to be the most powerful cancer preventer and inhibitor of established cancers), and K-2 (essential for cancer) every day, alongside calcium and magnesium minerals, lecithin, Omega 3-6-9 (fish oil), and Brite Eyes (antioxidant formula). In addition, I take DHEA (this hormone is said to have the broadest application against cancers of all sorts), co-enzyme Q10, Alpha Lipoic Acid, and carotenoid. I also take melatonin, which is not only a sleep aid, but appears to have anticancer properties. I'm covering all my bases.

As you swallow your medications and supplements, Dr. Joyce Whitely Hawkes, suggests that you bless them, and ask that they do the work intended for the healing of your body. And, as mentioned beforehand, I silently chant my mantra, "Transform. Regenerate. Renew," when I take my pills. The goal is to create optimal longevity and health. Expect the very best possible outcome. Deepak Chopra, M.D. and David Simon, M.D. add: "When you consciously take your supplements, and anticipate their effectiveness, you empower their effects and enhance their benefits."

Decades ago, I read two magazine articles that said Roddy McDowall (the movie star, for those of you too young to know) took 90 supplements a day, and I was shocked, finally deciding that it must be a misprint. I always thought I took a lot of supplements, but when I read in *Knockout*, that Suzanne Sommers takes 60 different supplements daily (Yowzers!), I am satisfied with my meager lot of 20 meds and supplements together (that I take with spring water), spread throughout my day.

Talk to a trained dietitian, nutritionist, or nutritionally-oriented physician or health-care practitioner for recommendations in selecting products or quality companies. (Unfortunately, vitamin store clerks are forbidden by law to give you helpful guidance.) Buy some good books on nutrition and supplements, to find out what's best for you. (Avoid synthetic supplements, and those that contain artificial dyes.) Consider a 2002 report from JAMA (the *Journal of the American Medical Association*), which clearly states: "Most people do not consume an optimal amount of all vitamins by diet alone . . . It appears prudent for all adults to take vitamin supplements."

We view nutritional supplementation
as an insurance policy.
—Deepak Chopra, M.D. & David Simon, M.D

RELATIONSHIPS

Shared joy is a double joy;
shared sorrow is half a sorrow.
—Swedish Proverb

It's almost impossible to go through life alone. Treat yourself with the medicine of positive relationships: family, friends, and neighbors. ("*I only attract loving people into my life.*") Having a handful of close, nurturing friends is wonderful; individuals with whom you don't worry about being misunderstood, envied, or judged. Social ties and warm, healthy relationships are important. You need to hang out with those who truly care for you, and vice versa.

Having a strong support network affects not just your happiness, but your physiology, as well. If you don't have such a support network, go about the business of forming one, via a team, a therapy gathering, a church, or whatever. Treasure the important people in your life. If you are living in an isolated area, or you have recently moved, and don't know anyone, try online support groups (cancercare, cancer support community, caring.com, and such).

"I have come to think of community as a kind of vitamin. The experience of connectedness with others is as necessary to a full healthy life as the minimum daily amount of the essential vitamins is to a balanced diet," said Claude Whitmyer. Having family, friends, and community around you fills a fundamental need to belong, in which you feel connected, supported, and loved.

You don't need experts to tell you that toxic relationships contaminate your peace of mind and emotions, but scientists now tell us that they also affect your health, and shorten your life expectancy. "There is nothing more draining than holding grudges," says Arianna Huffington, while quoting Carrie Fisher: "Resentment is like drinking poison and waiting for the other person to die." When you're in a relationship that isn't working, you need to move on, instead of giving it six weeks, six months, six years, or six lifetimes, advises Dr. Yvonne Oswald. (Unfortunately, letting go isn't my strong suit.) Studies show that loved ones may affect your health even more than what you eat, how you exercise, and whether or not you have good or bad health habits. It turns out that studies show a supportive, tight-knit group can not only increase your happiness, but your life span, as well: *by seven years!*

That is another good reason to avoid toxic people and experiences.

Oddly, data suggests that close friendships may be even more health-inducing than having a spouse. Even one supportive person can make a huge difference. Plus, positive social interaction may also decrease the amount of medication you need, and help accelerate your recovery. So keep your loving relationships close. As Robert Fulghum reminds us, in his worldwide bestseller book, *All I Really Need to Know, I Learned in Kindergarten*: "When you go out into the world, it is better to hold hands and stick together."

The supreme happiness of life
is the conviction that we are loved.
—Victor Hugo

FORGIVENESS

You can't forgive the wrongs,
you can only forgive the wrongdoers.
—Rev. Deborah L. Johnson

"Unforgiveness . . . is the most common root of physical illness," says Dr. Doreen Virtue. "Forgiveness doesn't mean that you deny the other person's responsibility for hurting you, and it doesn't minimize or justify the wrong," states the Mayo Clinic. "You can forgive the person without excusing the act."

"To forgive is not to erase things, but to shift your relationship to them," explains Rev. Deborah L. Johnson. In the changing of such relationships, you are no longer bound by that energy. By giving that person so much time and energy, he or she has become the focal point of your awareness. And you have better places to direct your focus, now that you are dealing with cancer.

There are those who maintain that all dis-ease comes from a state of unforgiveness. They say that when you are ill, you need to look around, and check to see who it is that you need to forgive. Uh-oh. I know exactly who I need to forgive, and I have been putting it off for a long, long time.

In the spirit of total transparency, I admit that I am still dealing with the issue of forgiveness. According to the FBI, I am considered to be the longest-stalked person in the nation (50+ years). As such, I have a lot of forgiving to do, as I was on the receiving end of much unwanted attention: constant harassing phone calls, a barrage of threatening love letters, unwanted gifts left on my porch, under intermittent surveillance, various attempts on my life, a deliberate car crash, two kidnappings, and so forth. As such, I'm carrying around a lot of heavy, unwanted baggage, (Read: *The Bogeyman: Stalking and Its Aftermath*, by Dr. Sherry L. Meinberg; or watch the 12/12/12/ Premier Episode rerun of *The Bogeyman*, on the Investigation Discovery—I.D.—channel, "Someone's Watching," for particulars.) My husband has often observed that, "Being in a stalking situation is like having a chronic disease. You go to bed with it, and wake up with it." Reluctantly, I am still learning the lesson of forgiveness. Even knowing that forgiveness isn't about erasing the wrongs, or prior situations, I am having difficulty forgiving my stalker for my being the target of his negative behavior. After all, 50-plus years of life-threatening, stressful situations was something akin to riding a nonstop roller coaster, in terms of the highs, lows, curves, and occasional screaming, yelling, and crying; it was like being trapped in a foxhole, in wartime conditions. I maintained a bunker mentality, fighting a war unseen by others. This wasn't just about trouble; it was about survival. PTSD loomed.

It took a lot of my time, effort, energy, and money, not to mention the extreme freak-out fear factor—as well as the mental gymnastics regarding anger, blame, guilt, resentment, and bitterness involved—which caused me to endure even less mental and physical peace. Not only was I angry with him, but also at the alienation, separation, judgment, and apathy, I experienced, when I pleaded for help—to no avail—from the police, the courts, and the legislators (I was neither "protected nor served.") So I was furious with society's system. Thank goodness things have now improved in awareness for those groups, as well as the public at large.

As a direct result of my being under siege for all those years, my blood pressure was off the charts (when you are under constant stress, your blood pressure goes up, which means that your heart has to work too hard). Upon being brought to the hospital, none of the nurses believed their stethoscope findings, and thought they were broken. So they each tried four or five different stethoscopes, before they finally believed that my top systolic number was 300. No one could believe it, and I was called the "walking dead." I have taken blood pressure medication ever since.

Unfortunately for me, Louise L. Hay (diagnosed with "incurable" cervical cancer in 1977, and is still going strong 38 years later, in 2015) says that ". . . the very person you find it hardest to forgive, is the one YOU NEED TO LET GO OF THE MOST." With the clarity that comes from stepping back, and taking the long view, I know she is right.

As my stalker has since died, I am now zeroing in on the fact that he was a psychotic schizophrenic, with delusions of grandeur, and his thinking and reasoning abilities were not that of a *normal* person. ("As the twig is bent, the tree's inclined," said Alexander Pope.) With such an unbalanced and damaged brain, empty eyes, and disregard for animals and people, I don't like feeling any sort of connection with him. He had no remorse for any of the women he had beaten, or raped, or maimed. He had no sympathy, compassion, or empathy for anyone, as he had scrambled wiring for brains. His acts were so heinous, I realize now that he was tormented and suffering in ways that I can never understand. And, as Abraham-Hicks suggested, his cruelty was an extension of that pain. I am thankful that I survived that experience, and I am almost there, in terms of total forgiveness.

As mentioned earlier, when Dr. Wayne W. Dyer received his cancer diagnosis, he treated it as *healing information* being given to him, rather than focusing on the disease. As such, he decided to heal "any and all relationship conflicts." He determined to heal any disputes, disagreements, or arguments, by offering "massive doses of unconditional love to everyone, including all those who played a major part in any and all conflict dramas" that once defined his life. *What a positive example for the rest of us!* (Dr. Dyer is still actively writing and lecturing around the world, all these years later.)

Regina Brett, a cancer survivor, says life is too short to waste time hating anyone. She suggests that if you have anger or resentment you would like to be free of, if you pray for the person or situation involved, you will be free. Adding: "Sometimes when I'm really stuck, I have to pray for the *willingness* to pray for the person. It always comes." Good idea. Life is too short to harbor harsh memories.

And Carlos Warter, M.D., Ph.D. shares a short and easy prayer of radical forgiveness: "I hereby forgive all. May no one be punished on my account. I hereby forgive all. May no one be punished on my account."

One of the best benefits of forgiveness is that the heavy weight is lifted off your shoulders. You are able to stop obsessing over the incident(s) involved. Your blocked energies are freed, and your anxieties about the future relax. As Rev. Deborah L. Johnson says, "The shields go down, your joy comes up, and you perceive good all around." So, you and I can work on forgiveness together, to be totally free, and embrace our futures. Oprah Winfrey said that, "True forgiveness is when you can say, 'Thank you for that experience.'" And I have to admit that I'm not there quite yet, but I'm working on it; I'm close to that chapter in my life being completely over.

"Forgiveness and treatment may go hand in hand," says Daniel G. Amen, M.D., in his *Healing the Hardware of the Soul*. Understand—along with me—that the lack of forgiveness puts you at risk, which divides your focus. So, whoever you need to forgive, *forgive!,* in order to place all your energies on becoming healthy and cancer-free. "Forgiveness is a powerful act that is healing to *you*," says Dr. Caroline Myss. "Embrace the healing energy of forgiveness." Forgiveness brings a kind of peace that helps you move on with your life. And Joan Gattuso, a Unity minister and cancer survivor, has a whole chapter on forgiveness in her book, *A Course in Life*. She says that forgiveness is the price you pay for your own freedom. FREE AT LAST!

The weak never forgive.
Forgiveness is the attribute of the strong.
—Mahatma Gandhi

HUMOR/LAUGHTER

Laughter is an instant vacation.
—Milton Berle

A bumper sticker reads: Cancer is not funny. But laughter is the best medicine. Sir William Osler, M.D. (one of the four founding professors of John Hopkins Hospital) called laughter 'the music of life.' "Laughter makes the unbearable bearable, and a patient with a well-developed sense of humor has a better chance of recovery than a stolid individual who seldom laughs," Bernie S. Siegel, M.D., tells us. Good to know.

Experts agree that a sense of humor is an enormous asset. "Life goes easier if you think of it as a practical joke," observes Leslie Miklosy. Having a sense of humor is an enormous asset, when dealing with cancer. Research shows that just by smiling, you change the chemistry in your brain. Your smiles release a hormone called beta-endorphine—into your central nervous system—which transmits a positive message to your brain, and actually makes you feel better. (And strictly from an energy standpoint, a smile needs only 17 muscles, whereas a frown uses 43 muscles. Think about it.) Neale Donald Walsch suggests: "Smile a lot. It will cure whatever ails you."

Laughing relieves stress. Laugh it off. As Erma Bombeck said, "If you can laugh at it, you can live with it." Clearly, the antidote for your serious attitude is to warm up a bit by laughing at your situation, and laughing with life. Consider your life as a comic strip, and laugh your way through it. "Humor's most important psychological function is to jolt us out of our habitual frame of mind, and promote new perspectives," adds Bernie Siegel, M.D. Not only that, but Dr. Joseph Mercola, in his newest book, *Effortless Healing* (2015), says that merely enjoying a laugh is as good for your blood vessels as 15 minutes of exercise. Wow! That's my kind of exercise!

Recognize that "Laughter produces more energy than screams," as Rev. Deborah L. Johnson says. Laughter stimulates electrical impulses in all parts of your brain. It sharpens your thinking, enhances creativity, reduces stress, and increases energy, making you more productive, while giving you a sense of well-being, explains Sandra Anne Taylor, in her book, *Quantum Success*.

Have you laughed today? How long has it been since you had a good belly laugh? (January 24th is World

Belly Laugh Day. Mark it on your calendar.) Bennet Cerf said, "For me, a hearty 'belly laugh' is one of the most beautiful sounds in the world." How long has it been since you really whooped it up? Let go of your inhibitions. Rediscover your inner child. Find your funny bone. Spread joy. With such lightheartedness, you'll see that your dramas are gone, your traumas are healed, and your whole life can be seen through the eyes of your humorous perspective. Yogi Berra noted the same: "Laughter is the shock absorber that eases the blows of life."

Experts agree that finding something funny, anything amusing under painful conditions, is good. Laughter causes positive physiological changes in your body, rallying your body's natural defenses against stress, pain, and disease. If you can laugh when you feel terrible, there's hope. Work to discover laughter and joy. It doesn't matter what you laugh at.

Having fun assures that you are in a positive frame of mind. You loosen up and lighten up when you let go of your seriousness, which places you in a highly magnetic state. Remember the Law of Attraction: Energy attracts like energy. As Bob Doyle explains: "It does not attract 'good' energy, or 'bad' energy. It attracts LIKE energy." So be the best magnet you can be, to attract health and well-being. "Unless each day can be looked back upon by an individual as one in which he has had some fun, some joy, and some real satisfaction," said former President Dwight D. Eisenhower, "that day is a loss."

Laughter is said to be the best medicine for both your body and your mind. Know that optimism, happiness, and laughter affects your life expectancy—adding up to ten years longer. Of course, you have heard of Norman Cousins. He was the first person to write a health book from the patient's point of view: *Anatomy of an Illness: As Perceived by the Patient.* He had been diagnosed with a fatal illness. So he checked himself out the hospital, and stayed in his apartment for one month. Along with taking Vitamin C, he watched tons of funny shows and movies, and read newspaper cartoons and joke books, and even wrote his own jokes. All of which relieved him of his pain, and lengthened his life. When he went back to the hospital, he had no symptoms whatsoever. He had laughed himself to health. He calls laughter "internal jogging." Laughter is one of the great healers.

And Hunter Doherty "Patch" Adams, M.D. agrees. His websites indicate that he sees his responsibility as a doctor to treat the body and the spirit through laughter. (See the movie: "Patch," a 1998 semi-biographical comedy-drama, starring Robin Williams.) He is a physician, social activist, clown, and author. He founded the Gesundheit! Institute in 1971, which supports an annual clown trip each year, to some place around the world, to promote healing through laughter. Check out his website.)

Multiple studies show that your over-all appreciation and enthusiasm of your life affects your health outcomes. Scientific proof of the health benefits from humor can be seen as early as 1989, when the Journal of the American Medical Association published a study showing that laughter therapy has an *immediate* symptom-relieving effect. And Christiane Northrup, M.D., says that: "Joy and laughter replenish you at a cellular level, so go for the comedy in life, and not the tragedy." She further believes that ". . . when you lose your sense of humor, you lose your vitality. At that point, you're just waiting for the end to come." Yikes!

Deepak Chopra, M.D. and David Simon, M.D., tell us that: "Laughter is a symptom of spirituality. Laughter is the flow of love, coursing through your body. Laughter is the nectar of present-moment awareness."

The most wasted of all days
is one without humor.
—e.e. cumming

RELIGIOUS/SPIRITUAL

Feed your faith and
your fears will starve to death.
—Author Unknown

To be spiritually healthy means taking responsibility for yourself, states Dr. Anne Wilson Schaef. You know that you are more than your physical and biological existence. Reawaken a sense of the sacred in your life. The materialistic approach to life leaves you emotionally unfulfilled, and largely disconnected from a sense of meaning and purpose, as well as spiritually empty, Shakti Gawain maintains. And Dr. Gay Hendricks, agrees: "Your inner life must be fed and nurtured as much as your physical body." Take this opportunity and use your cancer experience to grow spiritually and emotionally. Seek, discover, recognize, and embrace the divinity in you.

Daniel G. Amen, M.D. found that "the more patients were connected to their religious faith, whether

Catholic, Protestant, Jewish, Buddhist, or Muslim, the healthier they seemed to be as a whole." He further adds that studies "demonstrate how faith and religious connection have a healing impact on brain function." Other studies indicate that individuals with a strong religious faith, or who consider themselves to be spiritual, are more resistant to major illnesses, and recover faster from surgery, and live longer, than people with no religious faith. And, the more time that is spent in religious activities correlates with more satisfaction and overall happiness. (Keep in mind that the spirit world is nondenominational.) "The form your faith takes is less important than the love it imparts," adds Judith Orloff, M.D.

As such, resolving spiritual issues can significantly support your recovery from cancer, treatments, surgery, and emotional trauma. Dr. Joyce Whiteley Hawkes (an internationally respected research biophysicist, author, and healer) assures us that when patients combine spiritual and medical therapies, they report the best and most reliable results, saying, "Profound healing is possible as cell and soul connect."

Doctors are also saying that an active spiritual life plays a role in your cancer survival. Indeed. Andreas Moritz says, in *Knockout*, that ". . . spiritual health . . . plays at least as important a role in cancer as physical and emotional reasons do." As such, doctors are recommending some form of spiritual renewal and inspiration for patients to incorporate in their lives, suggesting: (1) Prayer; (2) Reading uplifting or comforting scriptures, spiritual, or metaphysical books; (3) Exploring the mutual truths and spiritual teachings of others; (4) Attending weekly religious services; and, (5) Involvement with a faith community.

Some patients may simply commune with nature, while for others the spiritual life may be represented through lecture or spiritual functions, meditation, yoga, tai chi, or gardening, inspiring literature, and uplifting music. (Dr. Masaru Emoto believes that good music has healing powers, which reach every one of your sixty trillion cells, and accelerates the recovery process.) "Say a rosary. Kiss a stone. Bow to the East. Chant a chant. Swing a pendulum. Test a muscle," suggests Neale Donald Walsch. Do what works for you. Christina Northrup, M.D., reminds us that your connection with the divine is always an inside job.

Louise L. Hay and Mona Lisa Schultz, M.D., in their book, *All is Well,* go so far as to say, "You must work to connect with the divine if you are going to heal." And, the advice from Dr. Carl Jung to a patient may hold true here: "Throw yourself wholeheartedly into any spiritual group that appeals to you, whether you believe in it or not, and hope that in your case a miracle may occur." As David R. Hawkings, M.D, Ph.D., adds, ". . . all illness should be reversible by changing thought patterns and habitual responses."

Whether you attend services in a church, synagogue, mosque, temple, lecture hall, house, or a gathering in nature, you can learn, pray, sing, and find fellowship. People who have been diagnosed with a life-challenging illness, who attend spiritual support groups, live on average, twice as long after diagnosis, said Marianne Williamson, in *The Gift of Change*. Later studies show, in *Mind Over Medicine: Scientific Proof That You Can Heal Yourself*, by Lissa Rankin, M.D., that by attending religious/spiritual services regularly, a larger social group interaction is involved, which would lengthen your life by seven and a half years (and almost 14 years for African-Americans). More than likely, you would be better able to find meaning in the face of loss or trauma, be more apt to overlook minor problems, while forgiving others, and simply be happier and healthier, than those who don't attend a community-based setting.

Allow the events of each day to take on spiritual significance. "Redefine 'spiritual life' so that it's your day-to-day life, lived well, with intention, integrity, and well-placed awe," suggests Victoria Moran. Look at your life through spiritual eyes. Open your mind, heal your heart, and soothe your soul. Your cancer may be a gift that increases your awareness of your true spiritual nature. Lisa Nichols tells us, "I looked back at each of the obstacles, dilemmas, and losses that *could have* taken me down, and asked the right question: What was the blessing of that experience?" See the value of your cancer experience in spite of your circumstances. Know that your personal story may spare others some grief. Studies have found that an active spiritual life clearly plays a role in coping with cancer, and quality of life issues.

Spiritual life is the bouquet, the perfume,
the flowering and fulfillment, of a human life.
—Joseph Campbell

PRAYER

When it's a glorious day I pray,
and it's a glorious day when I pray.
—Terri Guillemets

"Prayer is powerful medicine," states Dr. Caroline Myss. Over 300 scientific studies show that prayer works. Understand that prayer has an extremely beneficial effect on health. Experience an awareness of your higher self, by joining your mind, emotions, and spirit, in prayer, as a means of healing your body. Work to heal your whole self. You needn't belong to any religious or spiritual group to pray. Anyone can pray, at any time, anywhere, and anyhow. You don't need a go-between.

"Prayer is a concrete, measurable, and directive force in creation. Prayer is real. *To pray is to do something!"* Gregg Braden explains. View prayer as an opportunity to participate in the creative process of your life.

Healing Words, by Larry Dossey, M.D., documents both scientific and medical research about the remarkable power of prayer. And while one person's prayers alone can heal any condition, there is much evidence that group prayers can work wonders. Betty J. Eadie says that ". . . the power of prayer is the greatest gift that we have for any situation." She further discusses how one prayer is like a single light beam going straight to heaven, whereas the prayers of like-minded people forge a huge rope of bundled light beams shining upon heaven, which is even more powerful.

Numerous prayer studies agree, showing that prayer has a statistically significant healing effect, regardless of whether the patient knows about the prayers. And Carlos Warter, M.D., Ph.D., points out that the combined energy of your prayers, your physician's prayers, and the prayers of family, friends, neighbors, and strangers, complement your medical procedures and treatments—with no extra cost, and no harmful side effects.

Prayer heals. Prayer works. No matter what kind of prayer, in whatever language, you choose. There is no one-way to pray. This is not a one-size fits all experience. There are no hard and fast rules to follow. There is no right or wrong method to use. There is no particular way to pray. Understand that it's the *intention* that matters, not the length of the prayers.

There are, however, several categories of prayer, as Braden tells us: Colloquial prayers (in your own words), petitionary prayers, ritualistic prayers, meditative prayers, or a combination thereof. All must be based on *feeling*. Know and *feel* that your prayers have been heard, and have been answered. And hold that thought. Be surrounded or enveloped by what you desire. Show thoughts of appreciation and gratitude when you end your prayer. It is said that feeling *is* the prayer. Feel it in you heart. "Prayer," Braden continues, "is, to us, as water is to the seed of a plant."

Find a way to clear your powerful emotions of fear, hurt, anger, and frustration *before* you pray. It is said that your emotional state during prayer determines the kind of blueprint you create. You are looking for a sense of healing and peace. So prepare your mind and heart *before* you begin your prayers. Suspend any negative thoughts. Offer your prayers from a position of strength and clarity. Ask for and see yourself as living a long, healthy and vital life.

Dan Millman advises, ". . . pray as if everything depends on God, but act as if everything depends on you. Your actions make all the difference." Choose the outcome you want to experience.

David Cameron Gikandi explains that to pray without ceasing is not something you do just once a day, at a particular time. "It is something that becomes a lifestyle. It is going through the whole day, every day, with such focused intention for all your life's desires, with certainty, detachment, and gratitude. Prayer is meant to be active, ever present, and part of normal wakefulness."

Robert Arnot, M.D., explains that. "Morning prayers allow you to plan your day. Midday prayers give you a running assessment of how things are going. Night prayers allow you to reflect on what you have done right or wrong, and to think about how you might do better tomorrow." Understand that the quality of your prayers is not measured in length, or time, but in *intention.*

Joe Dispenza, D.C., says that we should surrender to the outcome of our prayers "to such a degree that we live as if our prayers were already answered." He further states: "Maybe it's not so important that we pray rigorously every day to have our prayers answered, but that we instead get up from our meditations as if our prayers have *already* been answered." ("*I am already healed.*") Mike Dooley agrees: "Pray in 'thank-yous' for stuff you haven't yet received or experienced (but as if you already had)." And Meister Eckhart—the 14th-century Catholic mystic—wrote, "If the only prayer you ever say in your entire life is 'Thank you,' that would be enough." (Quoted by "The American Lama," Lama Surya Das, in his book, *The Big Questions.*)

Lisa Nichols (CEO of Motivating the Masses) suggests that you praise and bless everything in your life! Bless everyone and everything. Pray for all, including yourself. Especially yourself. When you do so, you are on the highest frequency of love. And Gregg Braden goes so far as to say that, "Prayer may be the single most powerful force in creation."

Prayer is like pouring
hot water on an ice cube,
melting the cold and encrusted thought forms
that surround our hearts.
—Marianne Williamson

SURRENDER

"Turning it over" is a skill
as necessary for living
as for making pancakes.
—Victoria Moran

"One of the most liberating and empowering decisions you can make is the choice to let go," says Sandra Anne Taylor. Release old temptations.

You no longer need to be focused on the formidable mountain of cancer situated just outside the back door of your mind. If you are struggling through tough times, and just the thought of potential problems down the road is causing you to feel troubled, anxious, and burdened with despair, and if your worries seem to be running away with you, recognize that your cancer mountain is effectively blocking your way. Victoria Moran suggests that you need to surrender, to turn your problems and woes over to a Higher Power. This leaves you free to do what needs to be done to keep your life on track, while the new rule takes affect: God takes care of the mountain; you take care of your life. Focus your attention on the health improvements you desire.

If your belief system includes a personal God, let Him, Her, or Spirit, take over, when your challenge seems too overwhelming to deal with. When your cancer worries become too foreboding or too daunting, and they begin to resemble Pike's Peak, surrender your stress to a Higher Power: Give it up. Turn it over. Loosen your grip. Let it go. It is the healthiest thing you can do, as this release of pressure will lead to inner peace. There is freedom in your surrender. Sandra Anne Taylor says that you tend to think about the same issues over and over again. When you catch yourself thinking negative thoughts, she suggests that you say affirmations instead. ("I can let this go," or "I do not have to think this way any longer," or "I choose to release worry and frustration," or simply, "Release, release, release," or "Erase, erase, erase," or "*CANCEL!*").

Let God, the Great Unseen, the First Creator, or your Supreme Being, Source Energy, the Universe, or your Higher Self deal with it, while you focus on what you can handle, what's right in front of you today, one day at a time. Letting go releases old limitations. Surrender into how things are, rather than fighting it. Remain focused in the NOW. Worrying about the future, or the past, distracts you from the present. Stay in the NOW. "Let go, and let God," is often said.

In the same way that you turn away from temptation, turn away from your fears, and simply choose something different. Turn towards health and wellness. Remember, you bring about what you think about. "What you resist persists," offers Neale Donald Walsch. "What you most fear is what will most plague you. Fear will draw it to you like a magnet." And since you have already given over your doubts and worries and fears about cancer, don't rekindle them. Keep your eye on what's right in your world. Life is a process of creation. You are creating yourself anew. Have a grander vision. "Be patient, and trust in the Divine timeline," says Sandra Anne Taylor. Think only good, see only good, and expect only good, knowing that the Great Goodness has your back. Expect the best results possible, as you continue to do what you can, when you can, where you can, and however much you can. Center your attention on joy.

Just keep plugging along, with love in your heart, doing what needs to be done. Let no intimidating, negative thoughts weigh you down, knowing that a higher force is dealing with your mountain. As you are working through your days, committed to doing what needs to be done, your cancer mountain will start to erode. And your enormous obstacle won't seem that large, anymore.

To place something in the hands of God
is to give it over, mentally,
to the care and protection of the
beneficence of the universe.
—Marianne Williamson

GRATITUDE

My cancer scare changed my life.
I'm grateful for every new, healthy day I have.
—Olivia Newton-John

See value in each and every experience. Consider your cancer as a tool for growth and self-knowledge. "Any challenge put in your path, expands your awareness, and lifts your vibrational frequency," explains L.D. Thompson. Neale Donald Walsch agrees, saying, "There is a benefit and a blessing hidden in the folds of every experience and every outcome . . . including any "bad" thing that may be happening to you right now." He further adds ". . . that nothing is as bad as it seems. Nothing." And Robin Norwood says that the more you focus on your blessings, the lighter your burdens become. Stay in a state of appreciation—constant, continual, and chronic.

> *You say grace before meals. All right. But I say grace before the concert and the opera, and grace before the play and pantomime, and grace before I open a book, and grace before sketching, painting, swimming, fencing, boxing, walking, playing, dancing and grace before I dip the pen in ink.*
>
> —G. K. Chesterton (1874-1936)

Be in a persistent, perpetual state of gratitude. An attitude of gratitude is a lifestyle—a way of living; a way of being. No matter what shows up, you are in a position to deal with it. Victoria Moran says, "Say thanks for every day that's dazzling, every day that's good enough, and every day that you just make it through. Something else is always on the way." *("I give thanks for my ability to choose my thoughts, my attitudes, and my response to cancer.")* Regina Brett shares: "The night before my 45th birthday, I couldn't sleep. I felt so grateful to get to turn 45. Two of my aunts died of breast cancer before turning 45. I got breast cancer at 41, so I felt lucky to get to grow old." Understand that: "If you practice gratitude a little, you life will change a little," explains Rhonda Byrne. "If you practice gratitude a lot every day, your life will change dramatically, and in ways that you can hardly imagine."

> *We give thanks for the opportunity to heal and old injury, to close an old wound, to alter an old pattern, to shift an old reality, to release an old story, to change an old idea, and to create a new experience of Self and Life.*
>
> —Marianne Williamson

Feel appreciation and satisfaction with who, what, and where you are in life, regardless of your cancer situation. Eagerly anticipate your future. Mike Dooley suggests that you toss thanks around like rice at a wedding. Without gratitude, you may be focusing on what's wrong in your life, or what's missing in your life, rather than what's right in your life, and what you already have. "We often take for granted the very things that most deserve our gratitude," says Cynthia Ozick. Charles Dickens said it best: "Reflect upon your present blessings of which every man has plenty; not on your past misfortunes of which all men have some." (Remember: Whatever you focus on expands.) Lip service doesn't count. Your gratitude must be deep and heartfelt.

"Whatever our individual troubles and challenges may be, it's important to pause every now and then to appreciate all that we have, on every level. We need to literally 'count our blessings,' give thanks for them, allow ourselves to enjoy them, and relish the experience of prosperity we already have," says Shakti Gawain.

All your life, you've no doubt heard the words: "Count your blessings." Actually do it! At the dinner table, a little ritual could be that each member of the family might share the best thing that happened to them that day. Or just before you go to sleep at night, consider all the good that has happened to you that day. Then, wake up to a fresh, new day: "When you arise in the morning, think of what a privilege it is to be alive, to think, to enjoy, to love," Marcus Aurelius recommended. Joan Rivers suggested that you keep a notebook, in which you record three simple things that you are grateful for, each day. Such as, "I have a warm winter coat," or "I have indoor plumbing," or "My dog greeted me when I got home," to see the good things that surround you. Dr. Masaru Emoto encourages all to feel gratitude for the water that makes life possible. Willie Nelson said, "When I started counting my blessings, my whole life turned around." And when Dr. Albert Einstein gave thanks, he thought about *why* he was grateful.

William Arthur Ward asks: "God gave you a gift of 86,400 seconds today. Have you used one to say 'thank you'?" (*"I am filled with thanks."*) Be thankful and grateful for every moment you have! Treasure it.

Ward goes on to say, "Gratitude can transform days into thanksgiving, turn routine jobs into joy, and change ordinary opportunities into blessings." And Dr. Robert A. Emmons, psychology professor at the University of California, Davis, has provided eight years of research regarding gratitude, in his book, *Thanks: How the New Science of Gratitude Can Make You Happier.* He clearly shows that "Gratitude is literally one of the few things that can *measurably* change people's lives."

Even Albert Schweitzer. M.D., Ph.D. (awarded the Nobel Peace Prize in 1952), had this to say on the subject: "Gratitude is the secret to life. The greatest thing is to give thanks for everything. He who has learned this has penetrated the whole mystery of life—giving thanks for everything."

And Byron Katie says that: "The litmus test for self-realization is a constant state of gratitude." So, while you are spreading thank yous to others, don't forget to show your appreciation to your personal doctor, and your oncologist. Dr. Emmons says that, "Appropriate displays of gratitude are an important element in any healing relationship, and become increasingly so, as medicine becomes more and more fragmented and techno-centered."

In addition, Emmett E. Miller, M.D., quoted in Louise L. Hay's book, *Gratitude: A Way of Life*, says that grateful people heal faster, and are able to eliminate harmful behaviors from their lives with greater ease, and that they are happier. He has noticed—over 20-plus years—that his patients who were grateful for his sessions and insights regarding their health and well-being, were the ones who did well, whereas the others were much slower to change. And in the same book, Sharon Huffman shares that ". . . feelings of gratitude release endorphins throughout the body, creating health."

Christiane Northrup, M.D., adds that, "Prayers of gratitude are powerful for wellness." Greg Anderson says that he sees gratitude as bringing about the most significant and rapid improvement in the lives of cancer patients than any other single action. (*"Thank you for my perfect health: inside and out." "Thank you for my healing." "Thank you for the deep and profound love in my life."*)

Feeling gratitude and not expressing it
is like wrapping a present
and not giving it.
—William Arthur Ward

CELEBRATE

Each day comes bearing its own gifts.
Untie the ribbons.
—Ruth Ann Schabacker

"By failing to give ourselves the time for celebration, in effect, we give no attention or value to what is most significant in our lives," say both Salli Raspberry and Padi Selwyn, in their book, *Living Your Life Outloud.*

Always *expect* something worthy of a celebration to occur, urges Joan Gattuso. Mike Dooley agrees: "Allow yourself to appreciate, indulge, splurge, and celebrate today." Each day is special. Don't wait for a special occasion to celebrate. Celebrate now! Make the most of it. Get up, dress up, and show up. Become your own cheering section! Your life is full of opportunities to celebrate. *("I survive and thrive.")*

Neal Donald Walsch encourages all to: "Celebrate the shifting of the sand." Embrace change. Each small victory gives you the courage to stretch a little further, and risk, add Rasberry and Selwyn. Each step along the way to a cancer-free existence is cause for excitement. Celebrate each and every one of your accomplishments, changes, and breakthroughs. Have a party in your mind, in quiet triumph, if nothing else. *("I choose joy!")*

See the gift of your cancer experience (what Lisa Nichols calls "gifts that come wrapped in sandpaper"). She says, ". . . some of my greatest challenges were my greatest blessings." And if you can't see it yet, remind yourself that there *is* a gift to be found, and look for it. Be like the mythical phoenix, rising from your cancer ashes, to a new healthy life. Acknowledge your growth, new understandings, and unshakable commitment. Know that by your return to wellness and life-affirming choices, you are a living bridge for the next person who finds him- or herself faced with a cancer challenge. The key is that many people may benefit from your experiences.

Even if the world isn't noticing your mini-successes, notice them yourself. Allow yourself a moment or so of congratulation. Pat yourself on the back. Give yourself a mental high-five. Have a Mardi Gras in your head. Recognize what you've learned along the way, in your cancer journey, and give a whoop of uncensored gratitude.

Give yourself an award of some kind, for all your hard work. Buy yourself a guilt-free gift. Splurge.

Indulge yourself. Do something to mark the occasion of your cancer remission. Buy flowers, plant a tree, or go out and do something fun. Give yourself time to sparkle, shimmer, and shine. Feel special on this special day.

And mark your calendar each year, to show your cancer survivorship anniversary. It is important to take the time to reflect, and consider what you have learned, and how you have changed, since your diagnosis. Celebrate with a fancy dinner, or choose a special place or event to mark said achievement. The date I choose to celebrate is when I survived my uncertain surgery. Some choose the date of their diagnosis, others choose the date of their first treatment, while most choose the day they finished their chemo and/or radiation treatments. Some celebrate all. And why not? Who cares? You are simply noting that you are still alive and kicking on this milestone date, and are moving on. (Check out the Cancer Survivors Network.)

Loretta LaRoche reminds us: "If life is to be enjoyed, then you need to really believe that enjoyment is what it's all about. You need to take note of the wonders around you every day. You need to celebrate." And, according to a TV rerun episode of *Castle:* "Facing death demands celebrating Life!" So breakout the noisemakers and funny hats, and dance to the music. You've no doubt heard this before, and you've no doubt read this before, and although it has been misattributed to numerous people, it deserves repeating:

Yesterday is history.
Tomorrow is a mystery.
Today is a gift.
That's why it is called the present.
—Alice Morse Earle

ENDNOTE

This isn't the end of the story.
It's just a twist in the plot.
—Victoria Moran

Refuse to see yourself as a victim. Adopt a defiant attitude! Resist pressure to conform. Create your own pathway to health. Understand that the lessons of your cancer experience are always positive, even if the physical experience is not. If you stand back far enough to get the big picture, as Dr. Eric Pearl and Frederick Ponzlov maintain, you will see that ". . . in every experience there is the germ of incredible wisdom—*if* it is harvested, *if* it is recognized." As such, your cancer and its side effects may not all be bad. *("I am open to this cancer experience, and all it has to offer me.")* Bernie S. Siegel, M.D. notes that, "An awareness of one's mortality can lead you to wake up and live an authentic, meaningful life."

Father Paul Keenan encourages all to wonder and appreciate ". . . how tragedies often deepen us, give us compassion and wisdom, help us to discover what is truly important, lead us in new directions and down new paths."

And L.D. Thompson assures us that ". . . every time you accept your life as it is, accept the traffic jam, accept the expense you did not expect, accept the medical report—you gain ground. When you embrace what is, and assign to it the value that you are gaining ground in your experience . . . and wisdom, it allows you to make a quantum leap . . ." Adding, "The more you are willing to push your boundaries, the more you are going to learn about yourself." What you focus on expands, so focus on what you want. Dwell on health.

Remember, the quality of your life is in your hands. Success comes from taking control. Know that if you change nothing, nothing will change. As you no doubt have heard before: Change your thoughts and you change your life. "Ultimately, each person chooses whether he comes out of the tumbler crushed or polished," said Elisabeth Kubler-Ross, M.D.

Cancer is a call to listen to yourself, to pay attention to what your body is telling you; to take care of yourself in all ways. Cancer can also be a catalyst for reevaluating your life, giving you the time to do some serious inner exploration. By the time of your cancer remission, cure, or conclusion, you will most likely have acquired a deeper understanding of yourself and your personal power, alongside a philosophical attitude that has made peace with either outcome. You may now have a new appreciation for life, whereas it might have been taken for granted beforehand.

Pema Chodron (the first American ordained Tibetan Buddhist nun and teacher, and now the founding director of the Gampo Abbey monastery in Nova Scotia—the first in the Western world—and a prolific author) shares a conversation with a dying friend, in her book, *When Things Fall Apart:*

> He said, "I didn't want this, and I hated this, and I was terrified of this.But it turns out that this illness has been my greatest gift." He continued, "Now every moment is so precious to me. All the people in my life are so precious to me. My whole life means so much to me." Something that was horrifying and scary had turned into a gift.

You, too, have undoubtedly made some positive changes along your heroic cancer journey. It could be that fear and intimidation don't play the same roles in your life anymore. Maybe you are no longer easily swayed or manipulated by others. Perhaps you have replaced your passiveness, and are now action-oriented, and are in the driver's seat when it comes to your own interests. Instead of remaining quiet, you now ask questions, and state your opinion on various matters. You may have made the conscious decision to replace depression and helplessness with hope and trust. Perhaps you are better at controlling your negative thoughts. You may have softened your critical, angry, and confrontational attitude. Maybe you have stalled your workaholic actions, and allowed more play and less stress in your life.

Instead of using your habits and addictions as a method to counteract or escape melancholy, stress, anger, boredom, and such, you are now making better decisions as to how to spend your time. And you are taking consistent action towards your goal of health and well-being.

Maybe your limited interest in diet and supplements has moved you to make more healthful choices. Perhaps you are now living a more active life, by having made significant changes to enhance your energy, by walking, moving, or exercising. Or you may have made some major life-style decisions and changes. Possibly you pay more attention to your feelings, and have a better handle on your emotions, having let go of whatever was eating you inside. And you are now paying more attention to your body, as well, and pampering yourself more.

Perhaps you now have a less judgmental and more forgiving heart. You may have enlarged your circle of friends, reconciled damaged relationships, or left those that are no longer a match for you. You may be more loving to family, friends, and neighbors, and have empathy that extends to your community and the world at large. In addition, your relationship with others (their observations and interactions with you and your undesirable cancer situation) will have added immeasurably to their own knowledge and understanding.

Maybe you are seeing the glass as half full, instead of half empty, enjoying a brighter, sunnier side of life. You more than likely have made a shift in your values, spiritual beliefs, and practices. It could be that you have changed your perspective as to what you want to do, where you want to be, and who you want to be with. Perhaps you have learned the high value of NOW, and are enjoying each day, no matter what happens. Or you may have discovered your power, or the depth of your strength.

If *any* or all of these things have changed for you, look at all the GOOD your cancer has brought you! Eventually, you will have gained a greater understanding of your body, mind, and spirit. Be thankful for your positive changes, as you dance into the rest of your days, weeks, and years. Ensure yourself a big-picture Hollywood success.

Take the words of Brendon Burchard to heart, when he suggests that you live full out every day—energized, engaged, and enthusiastic about living. He further says that you can have *fun* in anything you do—even dealing with lawyers. (To which I would add: even dealing with cancer.) Intend to live a long, happy, and useful life.

Let us end with the inspiring words from Regina Brett: "Life is a wild, wonderful journey. Chaos will come, calm will follow, and then it will start up all over again. The secret is to savor the ride. All of it."

May your life blast off,
and your joys multiply.
—Mike Dooley

REFERENCES

REFERENCES

INTRODUCTION:

American Association for Cancer Research Progress Report (2014). *Transforming lives through research.* Retrieved January 20, 2015 from American Association for Cancer Research, AACR Cancer Progress Report 2014.Clin Cancer Res 2014;20 (Supplement 10:SI-7112)

CANCER DIAGNOSIS:

American Cancer Society (2014, August 11). *What is cancer?* Retrieved on February 2, 2015 from cancer.org/cancer/cancerbasics/what-is-cancer

American Cancer Society (2014, January 23). What are complementary and alternative methods? Retrieved on February 22, 2015 from cancer.org/treatment/treatmentsandsideeffects/complement.. . ..cancer/complementary-and-alternative-methods-and-cancer-what-are-cam

American Cancer Society (2014, June 26). *Coping with your emotions.* Retrieved on March 2, 2015 from cancer.org/treatment/treatmentsandsideeffects/emotionalsid. . . ecopingwithcancerineverydaylife/a-message-of-hope-coping-with-emotions

Brett, Regina. *God Never Blinks: 50 Lessons for Life's Little Detours*. (New York: Grand Central Publishing, 2010). pp. 74, 78-80.

Brokaw, Tom. *A Lucky Life Interrupted: A Memoir of Hope*. (New York: Random House, 2015). pp. 15, 29, 31, 39, 48, 49.

Carroll, Lewis. *Alice in Wonderland*. (New York: HarperCollins, 1992).

Dyer, Wayne W., Ph.D. *Wishes Fulfilled: Mastering the Art of Manifesting*. (Carlsbad, CA: Hay House, 2012). p. 109.

Healthy Reply (2014). *Cancer symptoms – general signs and complications of cancer* (Parts 1, 2, 3). Retrieved December 27, 2014 from healthyreply.com/cancer-symptoms-general-signs-and-complications-of-cancer/

Keen, Sam, Ph.D. *Hymns to an Unknown God: Awakening the Spirit in Everyday Life*. (New York: Bantam Books, 1994). pp. 14, 278.

Komaroff, Anthony, M.D. (Dr. K). "Make your doctor visits count." Long Beach *Press-Telegram*, 11, April, 2015. p. D3. Print.

Know Cancer (n.d.). *Top ten most common types of cancer*. Retrieved January 8, 2015 from knowcancer.com/blog/top-10-most-common-types-of-cancer/

Mayo Clinic. Staff. *Cancer diagnosis: 11 tips for coping*. Retrieved April 17, 2015 from mayoclinic.

org/diseases-conditions/cancer/in-depth/cancer-disanosis/ART-20044544

MedicineNet. (reviewed 2014, December 22). *What are cancer symptoms and signs?* Retrieved January 7, 2015 from medicinenet.com/cancer/page4.htm

Nagourney, Robert A., M.D. *Outliving Cancer: The Better, Smarter Way to Treat Your Cancer.* (Laguna Beach, CA: Basic Health, 2013). pp. 55, 169.

National Cancer Institute (2013, July 1). *What are clinical trials?* Retrieved from cancer.gov/clinicaltrials/learningabout/what-are-clinical-trials

National Comprehensive Cancer Network (2015). *NCCN guidelines for patients.* Retrieved January 17, 2015 from nccn.org/patients/guidelines/default.aspxNBC News/Amanda Chan (updated, 2010, September 10). *The ten deadliest cancers and why there's no cure.* Retrieved January 8, 2015 from nbcnews.com/id/39102353/ns/health-cancer/t/top-deadliest-cancers-why-there/s-no-cure/#.VK7241qGm-1

National Cancer Institute (updated, 2013, July 1, 2013). *What are clinical trials?* Retrieved February 22, 2015 from www.cancer.gov/clinicaltrials/learingabout/what-are-clinical-trials

National Cancer Institute (updated, 2014, March 21). *Common cancer types.* Retrieved January 8, 2015 from cancer.gov/cancertopics/commoncancers

People.com (2015). *Tom Brokaw: how I found out I had cancer.* Retrieved May 17, 2015 from people.come/

article/tom-brokaw-camcer-how-he-found-out-new-book-lucky-life-interrupted-memoir-of-hope

Rankin, Lissa, M.D. *Mind Over Medicine: Scientific Proof That You Can Heal Yourself.* (Carlsbad, CA: Hay House, 2013). pp. 42-48.

Schaef, Anne Wilson, *Ph.D. Living in Process: Basic Truths for Living the Path of the Soul.* (New York: Ballantine Wellspring, 1998). pp. 20, 111, 130-131.

Selig, Paul. *The Book of Knowing and Worth.* (New York: Tarcher/Penguin, 2013). p. 121.

Siegel, Bernie S., M.D. *Love, Medicine & Miracles: Lessons Learned About Self-Healing from a Surgeon's Experience with Exceptional Patients.* (New York: William Morrow, 2002). p. 37.

Simonton, O. Carl, M.D., Stephanie Matthews-Simonton, & James L. Creighton. *Getting Well Again: A Step-by-Step Guide to Overcoming Cancer for Patients and their Families.* (New York: Bantam Books, Reissue 1992). pp. 114-126.

Somers, Suzanne. *Knockout: Interviews with Doctors Who Are Curing Cancer and how to Prevent It in the First Place.* (New York: Harmony Books, 2015). pp. 20, 155, 181, 227.

The Top Tens (2015). *Top ten deadliest types of cancer.* Retrieved January 8, 2015 from thetoptens.com/deadliest-types-of-cancer/

Virtue, Doreen, Ph.D. *The Lightworker's Way: Awakening Your Spiritual Power to Know and Heal.* (Carlsbad, CA: Hay House, 1997). pp. 16, 41, 47.

Williamson, Marianne. *The Gift of Change: Spiritual Guidance for a Radically New Life.* (San Francisco, CA: HarperSanFrancisco, 2004). p. 6.

CANCER STAGES AND GRADING:

National Cancer Institute (reviewed 2013, May 3). *Cancer staging*. Retrieved December 27, 2014 from cancer.gov/cancertopics/factsheet/Detection/staging

CANCER STATISTICS:

American Cancer Society (2015). *Cancer facts and statistics*. Retrieved February 8, 2015 from cancer.org/research/cancerfactsstatistics/index

Anderson, Greg. *Cancer: 50 Essential Things To Do.* (New York: Plume/Penguin 2013).

Cohen, Alan. *Relax into Wealth: How to Get More by Doing Less.* (New York: Tarcher/Penguin, 2006.) p. 105.

Dyer, Wayne W., Ph.D. *Wishes Fulfilled: Mastering the Art of Manifesting.* (Carlsbad, CA: Hay House, 2012). pp. 109, 112.

Fulghum, Robert. *All I Need to Know I Learned in Kindergarten: Uncommon Thoughts on Uncommon*

Things. (New York: Ballantine Books, 2003). pp. 21-22.

Kubler-Ross, Elisabeth, M.D., *The Wheel of Life: A Memoir of Living and Dying*. (New York: Scribner, 1997). p. 167.

Siegel, Bernie S, *M.D. Love, Medicine, and Miracles: Lessons Learned About Self-Healing from a Surgeon's Experience with Exceptional Patients*. (New York: William Morrow, 1986). pp. 20, 21, 32, 39, 41, 43.

CANCER CAUSES:

Anderson, Greg. *The Cancer Conqueror*. (New York: Andrews McMeel Publishing, 2000). Business Insider (2015, January 1). *Groundbreaking study reveals the main reason most people get cancer*. Retrieved January 1, 2015) from businessinsider. com/r-biological-bad-luck-blamed-in-two-thirds-of-cancer-cases-2015-1

Chopra, Deepak, M.D. *Unconditional Life: Discovering the Power to Fulfill Your Dreams*. (New York: Bantum, 1992). pp. 75, 99.

Dooley, Mike. *Leveraging the Universe: 7 Steps to Engaging Life's Magic*. (New York: Atria Books, 2011. pp. 30, 49, 77, 81, 82.

-----. *More Notes from the Universe: Life, Dreams, and Happiness*. (New York: Atria Books, 2008). p. 32.

Dyer, Wayne W., Ph.D. *I Can See Clearly Now.* (Carlsbad, CA: Hay House, 2014). p. 102.

Hawkins, David, M.D., Ph.D. *Power vs. Force: The Hidden Determinants of Human Behavior.* (Carlsbad, CA: Hay House, 2002). p. 218.

Hay, Louise L. *You Can Heal Your Life.* (Carlsbad, CA: Hay House, 2004). p. 158.

Komaroff, Anthony, M.D. (Dr. K). "'Bad luck' is a questionable explanation for cancer." Long Beach *Press-Telegram*, 7, Ap., 2015. p. 10. Print.

Maté, Gabor, M.D. *When the Body Says NO: Exploring the Stress-Disease Connection.* (Hoboken, NJ: Wiley, 2011). p. xi.

Myss, Caroline, Ph.D. *Anatomy of the Spirit: The Seven Stages of Power and Healing.* (New York: Harmony Books, 1996). pp. xii, 6, 20.

Norwood, Robin. *Why Me, Why This, Why Now: A Guide to Answering Life's Toughest Questions.* (New York: Tarcher, 2013). pp. 39, 100, 104, 105.

Pearl, Eric, Ph.D. & Frederick Ponzlov. *Solomon Speaks on Reconnecting Your Life.* (Carlsbad, CA: Hay House, 2013). pp. 124-125.

Siegel, Bernie S., M.D. *Love, Medicine, & Miracles: Lessons Learned About Self-Healing from a Surgeon's Experience with Exceptional Patients.* (New York: William Morrow, 2002). pp. x, 65-70.

Somers, Suzanne. *Knockout: Interviews with Doctors Who Are Curing Cancer and how to Prevent It in the First Place*. (New York: Harmony Books, 2015). p. 153.

COPING WITH CANCER

SELF CARE:

Abraham-Hicks Publications (2015, March 22). *Daily Quote* (Excerpted from the book: *The Vortex* on August 31, 2009). Retrieved March 22, 2015 from dailyquote@abraham-hicks.com

Anderson, Greg. *Cancer: 50 Essential Things To Do.* (New York: Plume/Penguin 2013).

-----. *The Cancer Conqueror: An Incredible Journey to Wellness*. (Kansas City: Andrews and McMeel, reprint 2000). p. 99.

Brainy Quotes (2015). *Regina Brett quotes*. Retrieved May 10, 2015 from page 1 brainyquote.com/quotes/authors/r/regina_brett.html

Brett, Regina. *God Never Blinks. 50 Lessons for Life's Little Detours*. (New York: Grand Central Publishing, 2011). pp. 98-101.

Campbell, Chellie. *The Wealthy Spirit: Daily Affirmations for Financial Stress Reduction*. (Naperville, IL: Sourcebooks, Inc.). p. 93.

CancerTreatment.com (2015). *Alternative cancer treatment.* Retrieved 4/7/15 from alternative.cancertreatment.net/

Chopra, Deepak, M.D. & David Simon, M.D. *Grow Younger, Live Longer: 10 Steps to Reverse Aging.* (New York: Harmony: 2001). p. 20.

Cohen, Alan. *Relax into Wealth: How to Get More by Doing Less.* (New York: Tarcher/Penguin, 2006). pp. 84, 94.

The Dalai Lama. *The Art of Happiness: A Handbook for Living.* (New York: Riverhead Books, 1998). p. 167.

Frahm, A.E. & D.J. (1997). *A cancer battle plan: six strategies for beating cancer, from a recovered "hopeless case."* (New York: Tarcher/Putnam, 1997).

Hay, Louise L. & Mona Lisa Schultz, M.D., Ph.D. *All is Well: Heal Your Body with Medicine, Affirmations, and Intuition.* (Carlsbad, CA: Hay House, 2013.) p.8.

Hay, Louise L. *You Can Heal Your Life.* (Carlsbad, CA: Hay House, 2004).

-----. *The Power is Within You.* (Carlsbad, CA: Hay House, 1991). pp. xv-xvi.

Howe, Huebert M. *Do Not Go Gentle.* (New York: Norton, 1981.)

Kubler-Ross, Elisabeth, M.D. *The Wheel of Life: A Memoir of Living and Dying.* (New York: Scribner, 1997). p. 15.

Maté, Gabor, M.D. *When the Body Says NO: Exploring the Stress-Disease Connection.* (Hoboken, NJ: Wiley, 2011). p. 95.

Mercla, Joseph, Ph.D. *Effortless Healing: 9 Simple Ways to Sidestep Illness, Shed Excess Weight, and Help Your Body Fix Itself.* (New York: Harmony, 2015). p. 20.

Moran, Victoria. *Creating a Charmed Life: Sensible, Spiritual Secrets Every Busy Woman Should Know.* (San Francisco: HarperSanFrancisco, 1999). pp. 156-157.

Morris, Barbara, R.Ph., *Put Old On Hold.* (Escondido, CA: Image F/X Publications, 2004.) pp. xiii-xvii.

Nagourney, R.A., M.D. (2013). *Outliving Cancer: The better, smarter way to treat your cancer.* (Laguna Beach, CA: Basic Health Publications).

Rankin, Lissa, M.D. *Mind Over Medicine: Scientific Proof That You Can Heal Yourself.* (Carlsbad, CA: Hay House, 2013). pp. 72-79, 162.

Simonton, O. Carl, M.D., Stephanie Matthews-Simonton, & James L. Creighton, *Getting Well Again: A Step-by-Step, Self-Help Guide to Overcoming Cancer for Patients and Their Families.* (New York: Bantam Books, 1992).

Siegel, Bernie S., M.D. *Love, Medicine and Miracles: Lessons Learned About Self-Healing from a Surgeon's Experience with Exceptional Patients.* (New York: William Morrow, 2002). p. 41.

Stoddard, Alexandra. *Living Beautifully Together.* (New York: Doubleday, 1989). p. 110.

Taylor, Eldon, Ph.D. *I Believe: When What You Believe Matters!* (Carlsbad, CA: Hay House, 2012). pp. 182-183.

Turner, Kelly A., Ph.D. *Radical Remission: Surviving Cancer Against All Odds.* (New York: HarperOne, 2014). pp. 45-74.

Virtue, Doreen, Ph.D. *The Lightworker's Way: Awakening Your Spiritual Power to Know and Heal.* (Carlsbad, CA: Hay House, 1979). pp. 5, 14.

Walsch, Neale Donald. *The Only Thing That Matters.* (Ashland, OR: EmNin, 2012). p. 28.

-----. *Conversations with God: An Uncommon Dialogue (Book 2)*. Charlottesville, VA: Hampton Roads, 1997). p. 98.

MIND/EMOTIONS:

Abraham-Hicks Publications (1998, September 5). *Daily Quote* (Excerpted from the workshop: Asheville, NC). Retrieved April 4, 2015 from dailyquote@abraham-hicks.com

Arnot, Robert, M.D. *The Biology of Success.* (Boston: Little, Brown, 2000). p. 187.

Chopra, Deepak, M.D. *Creating Health: How to Wake Up the Body's Intelligence.* (New York: Houghton Mifflin, 1991). p. 8.

Cohen, Alan. *Relax into Wealth: How to Get More by Doing Less*. (New York: Tarcher/Penguin, 2006). p. 43.

The Dalai Lama. *The Art of Happiness: A Handbook for Living*. (New York: Riverhead Books, 1998). p. 178.

Emoto, Masaru, Ph.D. *The Hidden Messages in Wate*r. (Hillsboro, OR: Beyond Words Publishing, 2004). pp. xvi, 77.

Gawain Shakti. *Creative Visualization: Use the Power of Your Imagination to Create What You Want in Your Life*. (San Rafael, CA: New World Library, 1995). p.29.

Hay, Louise L. & Mona Lisa Schulz, M.D., Ph.D. *All is Well: Heal Your Body with Medicine, Affirmations, and Intuition*. (Carlsbad, CA: Hay House, 2013).

Hay, Louise L. *Heal Your Body: The Mental Causes for Physical Illness and the Metaphysical Way to Overcome Them*. (Carlsbad, CA: Hay House, 1976).

Keenan, Father Paul. *Good News for Bad Days: Living a Soulful Life*. (New York: Warner Books, 1998). p.197.

Maté, Gabor, M.D. *When the Body Says No: Exploring the Stress Disease Connection*. (Hoboken, NJ: Wiley, 2011). pp.xii, 12, 92.

Myss, Carolyn, Ph.D. . *Invisible Acts of Power: Personal Choices That Create Miracles*. (New York: Free Press, 2004). pp. 207, 228, 245.

Northrup, Christiane, M.D. *Goddesses Never Age: The Secret Prescription for Radiance, Vitality, and*

Well-Being. (Carlsbad, CA: Hay House, 2015). pp. xiv, 55, 56, 116

Pert, Candace B., Ph.D. *Molecules of Emotion: The Science Behind Mind-Body Medicine*. (New York: Scribner, 2003). pp. 274-275, 285-286.

Rankin, Lissa, M.D. *Mind Over Medicine: Scientific Proof That You Can Heal Yourself*. (Carlsbad, CA: Hay House, 2013). p. 79.

Selig, Paul. *The Book of Knowing and Worth*. (New York: Tarcher/Penguin, 2013). p. 46.

Small, Gary, M.D. *The Memory Bible: An Innovative Strategy for Keeping Your Brain Young*. (New York: Hyperion, 2002). p.*68*.

Taylor, Sandra Anne. *Quantum Success: The Astounding Science of Wealth and Happiness*. (Carlsbad, CA: Hay House, 2006). p. 38.

Walsch, Neale Donald. *The Only Thing That Matters*. (Ashland, OR: EmNin, 2012). pp. 142-143.

-----. *Conversations with God: An Uncommon Dialogue. Book 1*. (New York: Putnam, 1995). pp. 187-189.

SELF-TALK:

Anderson, Belinda (2014, February 17). *14 mantras to help you build positive self-talk*. Retrieved April 5, 2015 from mindbodygreen.com/0-12637/14-mantras-to-help-you-build-positive-self-talk.html

Chopra, Deepak. M.D. *Ageless Body, Timeless Mind: The Quantum Alternative to Growing Old.* (New York: Harmony Books, 1993). p. 24.

Cohen, Alan. *Relax into Wealth: How to Get More by Doing Less.* (New York: Tarcher/Penguin, 2006). p. 176.

Dyer, Wayne W., Ph.D. *The Power of Intention: Learning to Co-Create Your World Your Way.* (Carlsbad: Hay House, 2010). p. 69.

Hicks, Esther & Jerry Hicks. *The Vortex: Where the Law of Attraction Assembles All Cooperative Relationships.* (Carlsbad, CA: Hay House, 2009). pp. 11, 21, 22, 27, 54.

Johnson, Deborah L., Rev. *Your Deepest Intent.* (Boulder, CO: Sounds True, 2007). p. 228.

Levine, Barbara Hoberman. *Your Body Believes Every Word You Say: The Language of the Body/Mind Connection.* (Fairfield, CT: Aslan Publishing, 1991). p. 49.

Lim, Evelyn (2008, July 15). *7 steps to positive self talk.* Retrieved April 5, 2015 from pickthebrain.com/blog/7-steps-to-positive-self-talk/

Oswald, Yvonne, Ph.D. *Every Word Has Power: Switch on Your Language and Turn on Your Life.* (New York: Beyond Words, 2008). p. xxvii.

Rankin, Lissa, M.D. *Mind Over Medicine: Scientific Proof That You Can Heal Yourself.* (Carlsbad, CA: Hay House, 2013). p. 21.

Scott, Elizabeth, M.S. (2014, December 15, updated). *How your attitude and self talk affect stress.* Retrieved April 4, 2015 from stress.about.com/od/optimismspirituality/a/selftalk.htm

DECIDE/DECLARE:

Hay, Louise L. *You Can Heal Your Life.* (Carlsbad, CA: Hay House, 2004).

-----. *The Power is Within You.* (Carlsbad, CA: Hay House, 1991). p. 21.

Johnson, Deborah L., Rev.*Your Deepest Intent.* (Boulder, CO: Sounds True, 2007). p. 189.

Rankin, Lissa, M.D. *Mind Over Medicine: Scientific Proof That You Can Heal Yourself.* (Carlsbad, CA: Hay House, 2013).

Miller, Carolyn Godschild, Ph.D. *Creating Miracles: A Practical Guide to Devine Intervention.* (Novato, CA: H.J. Kramer, 2006). p. 143.

Proctor, Bob. *It's Not About the Money.* (Toronto, Ontario, Canada: BurmanBooks, 2008). pp. 28, 33, 99, 110.

Shakespeare, William. "Measure for Measure", Act 1 Scene 4.

Walsch, Neale Donald. *Conversations with God: An Uncommon Dialogue (Book 2*). Charlottesville, VA: Hampton Roads, 1997). p. 111.

-----. *Conversations with God: An Uncommon Dialogue. Book 1.* (New York: Putnam, 1996). pp. 56, 92, 100.

Williamson, Marianne. *The Gift of Change: Spiritual Guidance for a Radically New Life.* (San Francisco, CA: HarperSanFrancisco, 2004). p. 113.

BELIEF:

Abraham-Hicks Publications (2010, November 1). *Daily Quote* (Excerpted from the workshop: *Getting into the vortex guided meditation CD and user guide*). Retrieved January 14, 2015 from dailyquote@abraham-hicks.com

Braden, Gregg. *The Spontaneous Healing of Belief: Shattering the Paradigm of False Limits.* (Carlsbad, CA: Hay House, 2008).

Cohon, Alan. *Relax into Wealth: How to get More by Doing Less.* (New York: Tarcher/Penguin, 2006). p. 13.

Dennis, Helen. "Doctor: Lifestyle Affects Growing Older." *Press-Telegram* [Long Beach, CA], 1 Feb. 2015, Health ed.: 4. Print

Dooley, Mike. *The Top Ten Things Dead People Want to Tell You.* (Carlsbad, CA: Hay House, 2014). pp. 157, 162.

-----. *Manifesting Change: It Couldn't Be Easier.* (New York: Atria Books, 2010), pp. 58, 66.

-----. *Even More Notes from the Universe: Dancing Life's Dance.* (New York: Atria Books, 2008). pp.15, 90.

Dyer, Wayne W., Ph.D. *You'll See It When You Believe It.* (Canton, MA: Arrow, 2005).

Gattuso, Joan. *A Course in Life: The Twelve Universal Principles for Achieving a Life Beyond Your Dreams.* (New York: Tarcher/Putnam, 1998). pp. 51-52.

Gawain, Shakti. *Creative Visualization: Use the Power of Your Imagination to Create What You Want in Your Life.* (San Rafael, CA: New World Library, 1995). p. 25.

Graziosi, Dean. *Totally Fulfilled: More Money, More Freedom, More Smiles, Less Stress.* (Tucker, GA: Visionary Publishing, 2006). p. 16.

Kubler-Ross, Elisabeth, M.D. *The Wheel of Life: A Memoir of Living and Dying.* (New York: Scribner. 1997). pp. 229, 233, 276.

Levine, Barbara Hoberman. *Your Body Believes Every Word You Say.* (Fairfield, CT: Aslan Publishing, 1991).

Lipton, Bruce, Ph.D. *The Biology of Belief: Unleashing the Power of Consciousness, Matter, and Miracles.* (Santa Rosa, CA: Mountain/Elite Books, 2005). pp. 123-144.

Orloff, Judith, M.D. *Second Sight.* (New York: Warner Books, 1996). p. 296.

Rankin, Lissa, M.D. *Mind Over Medicine: Scientific Proof That You Can Heal Yourself.* (Carlsbad, CA: Hay House, 2013). pp. xi-xxiv, 3-13, 39.

Schaef, Anne Wilson. *Living in Process: Basic Truths for Living the Path of the Soul.* (New York: Ballantine Wellspring, 1998). pp. xiv, 47.

Taylor, Eldon, Ph.D. (2015, March 10). *Proof that what you believe matters!* Retrieved March 10, 2015 from intouch@innertalk.com

-----. *I Believe: When What You Believe Matters!* (Carlsbad, CA: Hay House, 2012). p. 1.

Taylor, Sandra Anne. *Quantum Success: The Astounding Science of Wealth and Happiness.* (Carlsbad, CA: Hay House, 2006). pp 22-23, 82-83, 222.

Walsch, Neale Donald. *Moments of Grace: When God Touches Our Lives Unexpectedly.* (Charlottesville, VA: 2001). pp. 156-157.

-----. *Conversations with God: An Uncommon Challenge (Book 3).* (Charlottesville, VA: Hampton Roads, 1998). p. 110.

ACT AS IF:

Braden, Gregg. *The Isaiah Effect: Decoding the Lost Science of Prayer and Prophecy.* (New York: Three Rivers Press, 2000). pp. 91, 202.

Byrne, Rhonda. *The Secret.* (New York: Atria, 2006). pp. 113-117.

Dooley, Mike. *Manifesting Change: It Couldn't Be Easier.* (New York: Atria Books, 2010). p. 71.

-----. *More Notes from the Universe: Life, Dreams, and Happiness.* (New York: Atria Books, 2008). p.45.

Holmes, Ernest, Ph.D. *The Science of Mind: A Philosophy, A Faith, A Way of Life.* (New York: Tarcher/ Putnam, 1997). p. 147.

Moran, Victoria. *Creating a Charmed Life: Sensible, Spiritual Secrets Every Busy Woman Should Know.* (San Francisco: HarperSanFrancisco, 1999). p. 27.

Morris, Barbara, R.Ph. *Put Old On Hold.* (Escondido, CA: Image F/X Publications, 2004). p. 21.

LaRoche, Loretta. *Life is Short—Wear Your Party Pants: ten Simple Truths That Lead to an Amazing Life.* (Carlsbad, CA: Hay House, 2003.) pp. 146-151.

Michael, Todd, MD. *The Twelve Conditions of a Miracle: The Miracle Worker's Handbook.* (New York: Tarcher/ Penguin, 2004). pp. 127-134.

Williamson, Marianne. *The Gift of Change: Spiritual Guidance for a Radically New Life.* (San Francisco, CA: HarperSanFrancisco, 2004). p. 237.

STRESS MANAGEMENT

Anderson, Greg. *The Cancer Conqueror: An Incredible Journey to Wellness.* (Kansas City: Andrews and McMeel, reprint 2000). p. 41.

Chopra, Deepak, M.D. & David Simon, M.D. *Grow Younger, Live Longer: 10 Steps to Reverse Aging.* (New York: Harmony, 2001). p. 45.

Fred Hutch/McGregor, Bonnie, Ph.D. (2015) *Survivorship: stress management*. Retrieved 2015, January 29 from fredhutch.org./en/treatment/survivorship-strategies/stress-management.html

HelpGuide.Org. (2014, December) *How to reduce, prevent, and cope with stress*. Retrieved February 8, 2015 from helpguide.org/articles/stress/stress-management.htm

Hendricks, Gay, Ph.D. *Conscious Living: Finding Joy in the Real World*. (San Francisco: HarperSanFrancisco, 2000). pp. 47, 61-62.

Holmes, Ernest, Ph.D. *The Science of Mind: A Philosophy, A Faith, A Way of Life*. (New York: Tarcher/ Putnam, 1997). p. 145.

Johnson, Deborah L., Rev. *Your Deepest Intent*. (Boulder, CO: Sounds True, 2007). p. 201.

Ranklin, Lissa, MD. *Mind Over Medicine: Scientific Proof That You Can Heal Yourself*. (Carlsbad, CA: Hay House, 2013). pp. 76-79.

Simonton, O. Carl, M.D., Stephanie Matthews-Simonton, & James L. Creighton. *Getting Well Again: A Step-by-Step Guide to Overcoming Cancer for Patients and their Families*. (New York: Bantam Books, Reissue 1992). pp. 5, 32, 46-78, 93.

Turner, Kelly A., Ph.D. *Radical Remission: Surviving Cancer Against All Odds*. (New York: Harper One, 2014). pp. 138-139.

MedicineNet.com (2015). *Eight immediate stress busters.* Retrieved February 8, 2015 from medicinenet.com/script/main/art.asp?articlekey=59875

WebMD. (n.d.) *What happens when you are stressed?* Retrieved February 8, 2015 from webmd.com/balance/stress-management/stress-management-topic-overview

WebMD. (n.d.) *Stress management when you have cancer – topicoverview.* Retrieved 2015, January 29 from webmd.com/cancer/stress-management-when-you-have-cancer

Weil, Andrew, M.D. *Healthy Aging: A Guide to Your Well-Being.* (New York: Anchor Books, 2005). pp. 251-260.

ATTITUDE:

Abraham-Hicks Publications (2015, March 2). *Daily Quote* **(**Excerpted from the workshop: The Vortex on August 31, 2009). Retrieved on March 2, 2015 from dailyquote@abraham-hicks.com

Byrne, Ronda. *The Secret.* (New York: Atria Books, 2006). p. 141.

Das, Surya, Lama. *The Big Questions: How to Find Your Own Answers to Life's Essential Mysteries.* (New York: Rodale, 2007). p. 145.

Dennis, Helen (2015, May 24). Celebrating Older Americans Month. Retrieved May 24, 2015 from *Press-Telegram, D6.*

Dooley, Mike. *Notes fro the Universe: New Perspectives from an Old Friend.* (New York: Atria Books, 2007). pp. 9, 149.

Dyer, Wayne W., Ph.D. *I Can See Clearly Now.* (Carlsbad, CA: Hay House, 2014). p. 12.

Emoto, Masaru, Ph.D. *The True Power of Water: Healing and Discovering Ourselves.* (Hillsborrow, OR: Beyond Words Publishing, 205). pp. 29-30, 31, 34.

Gawain, Shakti. *Creative Visualization: Use the Power of Your Imagination to Create What You Want in Your Life.* (San Rafael, CA: New World Library, 1995). p. 29.

Hay, Louise L. and Friends. *Gratitude: A Way of Life.* (Carlsbad, CA: Hay House, 1996). p. 253.

James, Jacquelyn B., Elyssa Bensen, Christina Matz-Costa & Marcie Pitt-Catsouphes (2012, January). Insights on Activity in Later Life from the Life & Times in an Aging Society—Engaged as We Age. *Sloan Center on Age and Work.* Retrieved from Dennis, Helen (2015, May 24). Celebrating Older Americans Month. Retrieved May 24, 2015 from *Press-Telegram*, D-6.

Johnson, Deborah L., Rev. *Your Deepest Intent.* (Boulder, CO: Sounds True, 2007). pp. 106, 107, 114.

Khalsa, Dharma Singh, M.D. *Brain Longevity: The Breakthrough Medical Program that Improves Your Mind and Memory.* (New York: Warner Books, 1999). p. ix.

Michael, Todd, MD. *The Twelve Conditions of a Miracle: The Miracle Worker's Handbook.* (New York: Tarcher/ Penguin, 2004). p. 126.

Morris, Barbara, R.Ph. *Put Old On Hold.* (Escondido, CA: Image f/X Publications, 2004). p. 17.

Proctor, Bob. *It's Not About the Money.* (Toronto, Ontario, Canada: BurmanBooks, 2008). p. 43.

Rankin, Lissa, M.D. *Mind Over Medicine: Scientific Proof That You Can Heal Yourself.* (Carlsbad, CA: Hay House, 2013). p. 162, 137.

Taylor, Sandra Anne. *Quantum Success: The Astounding Science of Wealth and Happiness.* (Carlsbad, CA: Hay House, 2006). pp. 105-106.

Walsch, Neale Donald (2015, July 8). *I Believe God Wants You to Know.* Retrieved July 8, 2015 from today@ nealedonaldwalsch.

Warter, Carlos, M.D., Ph.D. *Recovery of the Sacred: Lessons in Soul Awareness.* (Deerfield Beach, FL: Health Communications, Inc., 1994). p. 225.

INTENTION:

Braden, Gregg. *The Isaiah Effect: Decoding the Lost Science of Prayer and Prophecy.* (New York: Three Rivers Press, 200). p. 27.

Burroughs, Tony. *The Code: 10 Intentions for a Better World.* (San Francisco, CA: Weiser Books, 2008). pp. 24, 29.

Dyer, Wayne W., Ph.D. *The Power of Intention: Learning to Co-create Your World Your Way.* (Carlsbad, CA: Hay House, 2010). pp. 68, 237, 231-246.

Emoto, Masaru, Ph.D. *The Hidden Messages in Water.* (Hillsboro, OR: Beyond Words Publishing, 2004). pp. *xxii, 142.*

Gikandi, David Cameron. *A Happy Pocket Full of Money: Your Quantum Leap into the Understanding, Having, and Enjoying Immense Wealth and Happiness.* (Bloomington, IN: Xlibris, 2008). p. 140.

Hicks, Esther & Jerry Hicks. *The Amazing Power of Deliberate Intent: Living the Art of Allowing.* (Carlsbad, CA: Hay House, 2006). pp. 47-52.

Johnson, Deborah L., Rev. *Your Deepest Intent.* (Boulder, CO: Sounds True, 2007). p. 21-29, 225.

McTaggart, Lynne. *The Intention Experiment: Using Your Thoughts to Change Your Life and the World.* (New York: Free Press, 2007).

Taylor, Eldon, Ph.D. *What Does That Mean? Exploring Mind, Meaning, and Mysteries.* (Carlsbad, CA: Hay House, 2010). p. 175.

Taylor, Sandra Anne. *Quantum Success: The Astounding Science of Wealth and Happiness.* (Carlsbad, CA: Hay House, 2006). pp. 56-57, 93-101.

Virtue, Doreen, Ph.D. *The Lightworker's Way: Awakening Your Spiritual Power to Know and Heal.* (Carlsbad, CA: Hay House, 1997). p. 123.

Warter, Carlos, M.D., Ph.D. *Recovery of the Sacred: Lessons in Soul Awareness.* (Deerfield Beach, FL: Health Communications, 1994). p. 90.

AFFIRMATIONS:

Arnot, Robert, M.D. *The Biology of Success.* (Boston: Little, Brown, 2000). p 182.

Braden, Gregg. *The Isaiah Effect: Decoding the Lost Science of Prayer and Prophecy.* (New York: Three Rivers Press, 200). p. 151.

Gawain, Shakti. *Creative Visualization: Use the Power of Your Imagination to Create What You Want in Your Life.* (San Rafael, CA: New World Library, 1995). pp. 42-50.

Gikandi, David Cameron. *A Happy Pocket Full of Money: Your Quantum Leap into the Understanding, Having, and Enjoying Immense Wealth and Happiness.* (Bloomington, IN: Xlibris, 2008). pp. 54, 58, 107, 210.

Hay, Louise L. & Mona Lisa Schulz, *All is Well: Heal Your Body with Medicine, Affirmations, and Intuition.* (Carlsbad, CA: Hay House, 2013).

Hay, Louise L. *You Can Heal Your Life.* (Carlsbad, CA: Hay House, 2004). p. 57.

Keenan, Father Paul. *Good News for Bad Days: Living a Soulful Life.* (New York: Warner Books, 1998). p. 140.

Kortge, Carolyn Scott. *The Spirited Walker: Fitness Walking for Clarity, Balance and Spiritual Connection.*

(San Francisco: Harper-San Francisco, 1998). pp. 47-67, 174.

Levine, Barbara Hoberman. *Your Body Believes Every Word You Say.* (Fairfield, CT: Aslan Publishing, 1991).

Maisel, Eric, Ph.D. *Affirmations for Artists* (New York: Tacher/Putnam, 1996).

Martin, Art, Ph.D. *Your Body is Talking; Are You Listening?* (Penryn, CA: Personal Transformation Press, 2008).

Taylor, Sandra Anne. *Quantum Success: The Astounding Science of Wealth and Happiness.* (Carlsbad, CA: Hay House, 2006). p. xiv, 24.

Thompson, L.D. *Fields of Plenty: A Guide to Your Inner Wisdom.* (Studio City, CA: Divine Arts, 2013). pp. 19, 21, 39.

MANTRAS:

Braden, Gregg. *The Isaiah Effect: Decoding the Lost Science of Prayer and Prophecy.* (New York: Three Rivers Press, 2000). pp. 90-93.

Dooley, Mike. *Leveraging the Universe: 7 Steps to Engaging Life's Magic.* (New York: Atria Books, 2011). p. 97.

Hay, Louise L. & Mona Lisa Schultz. *All is Well: Heal Your Body with Medicine, Affirmations, and Intuition.* (Carlsbad, CA: Hay House, 2013.)

Khalsa Dharma Singh & Cameron Stauth. *Brain Longevity: The Breakthrough Medical Program that*

Improves Your Mind and Memory. (New York: Warner Books, 1997). pp. 306, 374.

Korte, Carolyn Scott. *The Spirited Walker: Fitness Walking for Clarity, Balance and Spiritual Connection.* (San Francisco, CA: Harper-SanFrancisco, 1998). pp. 52-53, 54, 174, 188-189.

Neal, Terry L. *It's All Thought! The Science, Psychology, and Spirituality of Happiness.* (Lexington, KY: Amazon, 2009). pp. 210-211.

Walsch, Neale Donald. *Conversations with God: An Uncommon Dialogue (Book 1).* (New York: Putnam, 1996). p. 179.

VISUALIZATIONS:

Anderson, Greg. *Cancer: 50 Essential Things To Do.* (New York: Plume/Penguin 2013). pp. 261-264.

Bach, Richard. *Jonathan Livingston Seagull.* (New York: MacMillan, 1970). p. 58.

Burroughs, Tony. *The Code: 10 Intentions for a Better World.* (San Francisco, CA: Weiser Books, 2008). p. 149.

Cohen, Alan. *Relax into Wealth: How to Get More by Doing Less.* (New York: Tarcher/Penguin, 2006). p. 15.

Dooley, Mike. *Manifesting Change: It Couldn't Be Easier.* (New York: Atria Books, 2010), p. 136.

-----. *Notes fro the Universe: New Perspectives from an Old Friend.* (New York: Atria Books, 2007). pp. 118, 185.

-----. *Even More Notes from the Universe: Dancing Life's Dance.* (New York: Atria Books, 2005). p. 94.

Dyer, Wayne, Ph.D. *I Can See Clearly Now.* (Carlsbad, CA: Hay House, 2014). pp. 73-76.

-----. *Manifest Your Destiny: The Nine Spiritual Principles for Getting Everything You Want.* (New York: HarperCollins, 1997). p. 66.

Fulghum, Robert. *All I Really Need to Know, I Learned in Kindergarten: Uncommon Thoughts on Uncommon Things.* (New York: Ballantine Books, 2003). p. 184.

Gawain, Shakti. *Creative Visualization: Use the Power of Your Imagination to Create What You Want in Your Life.* (Novato, CA: New World Library, 2002). pp. 29, 60-61, 66.

Gikandi, David Cameron. *A Happy Pocket Full of Money: Your Quantum Leap into the Understanding, Having, and Enjoying Immense Wealth and Happiness.* (Bloomington, IN: Xlibris, 2008). p. 48.

Maltz, Maxwell, M.D. *Psycho-Cybernetics.* (New York: Pocket Books, 1989 reprint).

Michael, Todd, M.D. *The Twelve Conditions of a Miracle: The Miracle Worker's Handbook* (New York: Tarcher/ Penguin), p. 138.

Proctor, Bob. *It's Not About the Money.* (Toronto, Ontario, Canada: BurmanBooks, 2008). p. 74.

Siegel, Bernie S., M.D. *Love, Medicine & Miracles: Lessons Learned About Self-Healing from a Surgeon's Experience with Exceptional Patients.* (New York: William Morrow, 2002). pp. 152- 156.

Simonton, O. Carl, M.D., Stephanie Matthews-Simonton, & James L. Creighton. *Getting Well Again: A Step-by-Step Guide to Overcoming Cancer for Patients and their Families.* (New York: Bantam Books, Reissue 1992). pp. 106, 136-150.

Taylor, Eldon, *Ph.D. I Believe: When What You Believe Matters!* (Carlsbad, CA: Hay House, 2012). pp. 22, 132-134.

Taylor, Sandra Anne. *Quantum Success: The Astounding Science of Wealth and Happiness.* (Carlsbad, CA: Hay House, 2006). pp. 80-81, 159, 211-212.

-----. *What Does That Mean? Exploring Mind, Meaning, and Mysteries.* (Carlsbad, CA: Hay House, 2010). p. 128.

Thompson, L.D. *Fields of Plenty: A Guide to Your Inner Wisdom.* (Studio City, CA: Divine Arts, 2013). pp. 54, 57, 225.

Walsch, Neale Donald (2015, April 24). *I Believe God Wants You to Know.* Retrieved April 24, 2015 from today@nealedonaldwalsch.com

Weil, Andrew, M.D. *Healthy Aging: A Guide to Your Well-Being.* (New York: Anchor Books, 2005). pp. 258-260.

EXERCISE/MOVEMENT:

Arnot, Robert, M.D. *The Biology of Success*. (Boston: Little, Brown, & Company, 2000). pp. 72, 66- 81.

Dyer, Wayne W., Ph.D. *Your Sacred Self: Making the Decision to be Free*. (New York: HarperCollins, 1995). p. 264.

Kortge, Carolyn Scott. *The Spirited Walker: Fitness Walking for Clarity, Balance and Spiritual Connection*. (San Francisco: Harper-SanFrancisco, 1998).

Millman, Dan. *Living on Purpose: Straight Answers to Life's Tough Questions*. (Novato, CA: New World Library, 2000). pp. 93, 165.

Northrup, Christiane, M.D. *Goddesses Never Age: The Secret Prescription for Radiance, Vitality, and Well-Being*. (Carlsbad, CA: Hay House, 2015). pp. 265-266, 271.

Simonton, O. Carl, M.D., Stephanie Matthews-Simonton, & James L. Creighton. *Getting Well Again: A Step-by-Step Guide to Overcoming Cancer for Patients and their Families*. (New York: Bantam Books, Reissue 1992). pp. 108, 220-227.

Small, Gary, M.D. *The Memory Bible: An Innovative Strategy for Keeping Your Brain Young*. (New York: Hyperion, 2002). pp. 69, 166.

Weil, Andrew, M.D. *Healthy Aging: A Guide to Your Well-Being*. (New York: Anchor Books, 2005). pp.224-225.

REST/RELAXATION:

Brilliant, Ashleigh, *Pot-Shot* card *#4254* (Santa Barbara: Copyright Ashleigh Brilliant, no date). www.ashleighbrilliant.com

Fulghum, Robert. *All I Really Need to Know I Learned in Kindergarten: Uncommon Thoughts on Uncommon Things* (New York: Ballantine Books, 15th Revised Edition, 25th Anniversary, 2004). p. 19.

Rankin, Lissa, MD. *Mind Over Medicine: Scientific Proof That You Can Heal Yourself.* (Carlsbad, CA: Hay House, 2013). pp. 14, 56.

Rasberry, Salli & Padi Selwyn, *Living Your Life Out Loud: How to Unlock Your Creativity and Unleash Your Joy.* (New York: Pocket Books, 1995). pp. 35-45.

Small, Gary, M.D. *The Memory Bible: An Innovative Strategy for Keeping Your Brain Young.* (New York: Hyperion, 2002). pp. 68-81.

Walsch, *Neale Donald (2015, July, 6, 2015). I Believe God Wants You to Know. Retrieved July 6, 2015 from today@nealedonaldwalsch.com*

Weil, Andrew, M.D. *Healthy Aging: A Guide to Your Well-Being.* (New York: Anchor Books, 2005). pp. 236-246.

SLEEP/NAPS:

Campbell, Chellie. *The Wealthy Spirit: Daily Affirmations for Financial Stress Reduction.* (Naperville, IL: Sourcebooks, Inc.). p. 93.

Chopra, Deepak, M.D. & Simon, David, M.D. *Grow Younger, Live Longer: 10 Steps to Reverse Aging.* (New York: Harmony Books, 2001). pp. 41-59.

Fulghum, Robert. *All I Really Need to Know, I Learned in Kindergarten: Uncommon Thoughts on Uncommon Things.* (New York: Ballantine Books, 2003). pp. 6, 95.

Harvard Medical School (n.d.). *Importance of sleep: six reasons not to scrimp on sleep.* Retrieved February 8, 2015 from health.harvard.edu/press_releases/importance_of_sleep_and_health

Health (n.d.) *Surprising health benefits of sleep.* Retrieved February 8, 2015 from health.com/ health/gallery/0,20459221,00.html

Huffington, Arianna. *Thrive. The Third Metric to Redefining Success and Creating a Life of Well-being, Wisdom, and Wonder.* (New York: Harmony, 2015). pp. 74-88.

Jung, Carl G. (translated by Richard & Clara Winston). *Memories, Dreams, Reflections.* (New York: Vintage Books, 1965).

-----. (translated by R.F.C. Hull). *Dreams.* (Princeton, N.J.: Princeton University Press, 1974).

Koch-Sheras, Phyllis R., Amy Lemley & Peter L. Sheras. *The Dream Sourcebook and Journal: A Guide to the Theory and Interpretation of Dreams.* (New York: Barnes and Noble Books, 1998). pp. xx, xv.

Meinberg, Sherry L., Ed.D. *The Bogeyman: Stalking and Its Aftermath.* (New York: Writers Advantage/ iUniverse, 2003). pp. 52-53.

Mercola, Joseph, Ph.D. *Effortless Healing: 9 Simple Ways to Sidestep Illness, Shed Excess Weight, and Help Your Body Fix Itself.* (New York: Harmony, 2015). pp. 175, 179, 186-188.

Milne, A.A., *Winnie The Pooh: original version.* (New York: Ishi Press, 2011).

National Sleep Foundation (n.d.*). How much sleep do we really need?* Retrieved February 12, 2015 from sleepfoundation.org/how-sleep-works/ how-much-sleep-do-we-really-need

Orloff, Judith, M.D. *Second Sight.* New York: Warner Books, 1996). p. 241.

Rasberry, Salli & Padi Selwyn. *Living Your Life Out Loud: How to Unlock Your Creativity and Unleash Your Joy.* (New York: Pocket Books, 1995). pp. 86-98.

Roizen, Michael F. M.D.: Cherly Powell, "Latest Cleveland Clinic Venture a Real Sleeper," *Akron Beacon Journal Online,* August 8, 2011, www.ohio.com

WebMD (2003, October 1*). How sleep affects cancer: Poor sleep alters hormones that influence cancer* *cells*. Retrieved February 11, 2015 from webmd.com/cancer/news/20031001/how- sleep-affects-cancer

NUTRITION:

Anderson, Greg. *Cancer: 50 Essential Things To Do.* (New York: Plume/Penguin, 2013). pp. 237-248.

Chopra, Deepak, M.D. & Simon, David, M.D. *Grow Younger, Live Longer: 10 Steps to Reverse Aging.* (New York: Harmony Books, 2001.) p. 78.

-----. *Creating Health.* (New York: Houghton Mifflin, 1991). pp. 25-28.

Frahm, Anne E. & David J. *A Cancer Battle Plan.* (New York: Tarcher/Putnam, 1970). p. 66.

Hay, Louise L. *Loving Yourself to Great Health: Thoughts and Food—The Ultimate Diet.* (Carlsbad, CA: Hay House, 2014).

Khalsa, Dharma Singh, M.D. *Brain Longevity: The Breakthrough Medical Program that Improves Your Mind and Memory.* (New York: Warner Books, 1999). pp. 198-222.

Mercola, Joseph, Ph.D. *Effortless Healing: 9 Simple Ways to Sidestep Illness, Shed Excess Weight, and Help Your Body Fix Itself.* (New York: Harmony, 2015). p. 41.

Morris, Barbara, R.Ph. *Put Old on Hold.* (Escondito, CA: Image F/X Publications, 2004). p. 41.

Pert, Candace B., Ph.D. *Molecules of Emotions: The Science Behind Mind-Body Medicine.* (New York: Scribner, 2003). p. 298.

Somers, Suzanne. *Knockout: Interviews with Doctors Who Are Curing Cancer—And How to Prevent Getting it in the First Place.* (New York: Harmony, 2009). pp. xvii, 20, 23, 24, 26, 145, 152.

Turner, Kelly A., Ph.D. *Radical Remission: Surviving Cancer Against All Odds.* (New York: Harper One, 2014). pp. 13-43.

Nagourney, Robert A., M.D. *Outliving Cancer: The Better, Smarter Way to Treat Your Cancer.* (Laguana Beach, CA: Basic Health Publications, 2013). pp. 29-30, 73-78.

Northrup, Christiane, M.D. *Goddesses Never Age: The Secret Prescription for Radiance, Vitality, and Well-Being.* (Carlsbad, CA: Hay House, 2015). pp. 227-259.

Virtue, Doreen, Ph.D. *The Lightworker's Way: Awakening Your Spiritual Power to Know and Heal.* (Carlsbad, CA: Hay House, 1997). p. 91.

WATER:

Anderson, Greg. *Cancer: 50 Essential Things to Do.* (New York: Plume/Penguin, 2013, 4th edition). pp. 130-131.

Emoto, Masaru, Ph.D. *Messages from Water and the Universe*. (Carlsbad. CA: Hay House, 2010). p. 38.

-----. *The True Power of Water: Healing and Discovering Ourselves*. (Hillsboro, OR: Beyond Words Publishing, 2005). pp. xii-xiii, 4, 13, 15, 96, 99, 103, 118, 121, 123.

-----. *The Hidden Messages in Water*. (Hillsboro, OR: Beyond Words Publishing, 2004). pp. xv-xxviii, 1, 43, 76-77.

Fulghum, Robert. *All I Really Need to Know I Learned in Kindergarten: Uncommon Thoughts on Uncommon Things* (New York: Ballantine Books, 15th Revised Edition, 25th Anniversary, 2004). pp. 90-92.

Highley, Rainey Marie. *The Water Code: Unlocking the Truth Within*. (Houstin, TX: Divine Macroverse, 2012). pp. 6, 20-21.

Mercola, Joseph, Ph.D. *Effortless Healing: 9 Simple Ways to Sidestep Illness, Shed Excess Weight, and Help Your Body Fix Itself*. (New York: Harmony, 2015). p. 38.

Northrup, Christiane, M.D. *Goddesses Never Age: The Secret Prescription for Radiance Vitality, and Well-Being*. (Carlsbad, CA: Hay House, 2015.) pp. 110, 247, 252.

Somers, Suzanne. *Knockout: Interviews with Doctors Who are Curing Cancer—And how to Prevent Getting it in the First Place*. (New York: Harmony, pp. 104, 160, 177, 222.

Turner, Kelly A, Ph.D. *Radical Remission: Surviving Cancer Against All Odds*. (New York" HarperOne, 2014). pp. 14, 19, 28-29, 32, 42.

Weil, Andrew, M.D. *Healthy Aging: A Lifelong Guide to Your Well-Being*. (New York: Anchor Books, 2005.) p. 307.

SUPPLEMENTS:

Anderson, Greg. *Cancer: 50 Essential Things To Do.* (New York: Plume/Penguin 2013). pp. 225-236.

Chopra, Deepak, M.D. & Simon, David, M.D. *Grow Younger, Live Longer: 10 Steps to Reverse Aging.* (New York: Harmony Books, 2001). pp. 45, 85.

Fletcher, R.H. & K.M. Fairfield, "Vitamins for Chronic Disease Prevention in Adults: Clinical Applications," *Journal of American Medical Association* 287, no. 23 (June 19, 2002): 3127- 29.

Frahm, Anne E. & David J. Frahm. *A Cancer Battle Plan: Six Strategies for Beating Cancer, From a Recovered "Hopeless Case."* (New York: Tarcher/Putnam, 1997.) p. 92.

Hawkes, Joyce Whiteley, Ph.D. *Cell-Level Healing: The Bridge from Soul to Cell.* (New York: Atria Books, 2006). pp. 123-124.

Hyman, Mark, M.D. The Blood *Sugar Solution: The Ultra Healthy Program for Losing Weight, Preventing Disease, and Feeling Great Now!* (New York: Little, Brown, 2012). pp. 215-227.

Khalsa, Dharma Singh, M.D. *Brain Longevity: The Breakthrough Medical Program that Improves Your*

Mind and Memory. (New York: Warner Books, 1999). pp. 49, 205-213.

Neilsen, Joan Amtoft- (n.d.). *Cancer, nutrition and supplementation*. Retrieved February 15, 2015 from healingcamcer.info

Somers, Suzanne. *Knockout: Interviews with Doctors Who Are Curing Cancer—And How to Prevent Getting it in the First Place*. (New York: Harmony, 2009). pp. 154-155, 228-251.

Turner, Kelly A., Ph.D. *Radical Remission: Surviving Cancer Against All Odds*. (New York: Harper One, 2014.) pp. 105-132.

Weil, Andrew, M.D. *Healthy Aging: A Lifelong Guide to Your Well-Being*. (New York: Anchor Books, 2005). pp. 197-216.

RELATIONSHIPS:

Fulghum, Robert. *All I Really Need to Know I Learned in Kindergarten: Uncommon Thoughts on Uncommon Things* (New York: Ballantine Books, 15th Revised Edition, 25th Anniversary, 2004). p. 6.

Huffington, Arianna. *Thrive. The Third Metric to Redefining Success and Creating a Life of Well-being, Wisdom, and Wonder*. (New York: Harmony, 2015). pp. 119-121.

Oswald, Yvonne, Ph.D. *Every Word Has Power: Switch on Your Language and Turn on Your Life.* (New York:Atria Books/Beyond words, 2008). p. 145.

Rankin, Lissa, M.D. *Mind Over Medicine: Scientific Proof That You Can Heal Yourself.* (Carlsbad, CA: Hay House, 2013). pp. 85-87.

Small, Gary, M.D. *The Memory Bible: An Innovative Strategy for Keeping Your Brain Young.* (New York: Hyperion, 2002). p. 180.

Stoddard, Alexandra. *Living Beautifully Together.* (New York: Doubleday, 1989). pp. 6, 12, 36-37.

Whitmyer, Claude. *In the Company of Others: Making Community in the Modern World.* (New York: Tarcher/Perigee, 1993). pp. xxiv-xxv.

FORGIVENESS:

Abraham-Hicks Publications (2015, April 28). *Daily Quote* (Excerpted from the workshop: Los Angeles, CA on January 31, 1999). Retrieved April 28, 2015 from dailyquote@abraham-hicks.com

Amen, Daniel G., M.D. *Healing the Hardware of the Soul: How Making the Brain-Soul Connection Can Optimize Your Life, Love, and Spiritual Growth.* (New York: Free Press, 2002). p. 105.

Brett, Regina. *God Never Blinks: 50 Lessons for Life's Little Detours.* (New York: Grand Central Publishing, 2010). p. 18.

Dyer, Wayne W., Ph.D. *Wishes Fulfilled: Mastering the Art of Manifesting*. (Carlsbad, CA: Hay House, 2012). pp. 109-110.

Gattuso, Joan. *A Course in Life: The Twelve Universal Principles for Achieving a Life Beyond Your Dreams*. (New York: Tarcher/Putnam, 1998). pp. 185-198.

Hay, Louise L. *You Can Heal Your Life*. (Carlsbad, CA: Hay House, 2004). pp. 8, 70.

Johnson, Deborah L., Rev. *Your Deepest Intent*. (Boulder, CO: Sounds True, 2007). pp. 227, 233.

Mayo Clinic. (n.d.) *Forgiveness: letting go of grudges and bitterness*. Retrieved April 16, 2015 from mayoclinic.org/healthy-living/adult-health/in-depth/forgiveness/art- 20047692?footprints=mine

Myss, Caroline, Ph.D. *Invisible Acts of Power: Personal Choices That Create Miracles*. (New York: Free Press, 2004). pp. 168, 198.

Northrup, Christiane, M.D. *Goddesses Never Age: The Secret Prescription for Radiance, Vitality, and Well-Being*. (Carlsbad, CA: Hay House, 2015). pp. 211-213.

Virtue, Doreen, Ph.D. *The Lightworker's Way: Awakening Your Spiritual Power to Know and Heal*. (Carlsbad, CA: Hay House, 1997). p. 250.

Warter, Carlos, M.D., Ph.D. *Recovery of the Sacred: Lessons in Soul Awareness*. (Deerfield Beach: FL: Health Communications, Inc., 1994). pp. 25-26.

HUMOR/LAUGHTER:

Anderson, Greg. *Cancer: 50 Essential Things To Do.* (New York: Plume/Penguin, 2013). pp. 189-190.

Chopra, Deepak, M.D. & David Simon, M.D. *Grow Younger, Live Longer; 10 Steps to Reverse Aging.* (New York: Harmony, 2001). p. 219.

Cousins, Norman. *Anatomy of an Illness as Perceived by the Patient.* (New York: Bantam, 1981).

Doyle, Bob. *Wealth Beyond Reason: Your Complete Handbook for Boundless Living.* (Victoria, BC: Trafford, 2001). p. 27.

Horn, Sam. *Tongue Fu! How to Deflect, Disarm, and Defuse Any Verbal Conflict.* (New York: St. Martin's Griffen, 1996). pp. 12-13.

Intenders of the Highest Good (2015, February 9). *A vision for humor.* Retrieved February 9, 2015 from visionalignmentproject.com

LaRoche, Loretta. *Life is Short—Wear Your Party Pants: Ten Simple Truths That Lead to an Amazing Life.* (Carlsbad, CA: Hay House, 2003). pp. 83-104.

Mercola, Joseph, Dr. *Effortless Healing: 9 Simple Ways to Sidestep Illness, Shed Excess Weight, and Help Your Body Fix Itself.* (New York: Harmony, 2015). p. 198.

Miklosy, Leslie. *Thinkerer: A Thinker Who Tinkers with Words and Ideas.* (College Station, TX: VBUV, 2015). p. 51.

Northrup, Christiane, M.D. *Goddesses Never Age: The Secret Prescription for Radiance, Vitality, and*

Well-Being. (Carlsbad, CA: Hay House, 2015). pp. 42, 323-325.

Seigel. Bernie S., M.D. *Love, Medicine, and Miracles: Lessons Learned About Self-Healing From a Surgeon's Experience with Exceptional Patients*. (New York: William Morrow, 1998). pp. 44, 143, 145.

Taylor, Sandra Anne. *Quantum Success: The Astounding Science of Wealth and Happiness*. (Carlsbad, CA: Hay House, 2006). p. 236.

Walsch, Neale Donald. *Conversations with God: An Uncommon Challenge (Book 3)*. (Charlottesville, VA: Hampton Roads, 1998). p. 163.

RELIGIOUS/SPIRITUAL:

Amen, Daniel G., M.D. *Healing the Hardware of the Soul: How Making the Brain-Soul Connection Can Optimize Your Life, Love, and Spiritual Growth*. (New York: Free Press, 2002). pp. 9, 17.

Anderson, Greg. *Cancer: 50 Essential Things To Do*. (New York: Plume/Penguin, 2013). pp. 204-209.

Arnot, Robert, M.D. *The Biology of Success*. (Boston: Little, Brown, & Company, 2000). pp. 193-196.

Dossey, Larry, M.D. *Healing Words: The Power of Prayer and the Practice of Medicine*. (New York: HarperOne, 1993).

Dyer, Wayne W., Dr. *Your Sacred Self: Making the Decision to Be Free*. (New York: HarperCollins, 1995).

Emoto, Masaru, Ph.D. *The True Power of Water: Healing And Discovering Ourselves*. (Hillsborro, OR: Beyond Words Publishing, 2005). p. 123.

Gawain, Shakti. *The Four Levels of Healing: A Guide to Balancing the Spiritual, Mental, Emotional, and Physical Aspects of Life*. (Mill Valley, CA: Nataraj Books, 1997). pp. ix, 7, 20.

Hawkes, Joyce Whiteley, Ph.D. (2015, March 12). *Cell-level healing: welcome to cell-level healing where science and spirit meet.* Retrieved March 12, 2015 from celllevelhealing.com/

Hawkes, Joyce Whiteley., Ph.D. *Cell-Level Healing: The Bridge from Soul to Cell.* (New York: Atria Books, 2006). pp. 30, 113.

Hawkings, David R. M.D., Ph.D. *Power vs. force: The Hidden Determinants of Human Behavior.* (Carlsbad. CA: Hay House, 2001). pp. 218, 220.

Hay, Louise & Mona Lisa Schultz. *All is Well: Heal Your Body with Medicine, Affirmations and Intuition.* (Carlsbad, CA: Hay House, 2013). p. 150.

Hendricks, Guy, Ph.D. *Conscious Living: Finding Joy in the Real World*. (San Francisco: HarperSanFrancisco, 2000). p. 69.

Johnson, Deborah L., Rev. *Your Deepest Intent*. (Boulder, CO: Sounds True, 2007).

Keen, Sam, Ph.D. *Hymns to an Unknown God: Awakening the Spirit in Everyday Life*. (New York: Bantam Books, 1994).

Korte, Carolyn Scott. *The Spirited Walker: Fitness Walking for Clarity, Balance and Spiritual Connection.* (San Francisco, CA: Harper-SanFrancisco, 1998).

Mercola, Joseph, Ph.D. *Effortless Healing: 9 Simple Ways to Sidestep Illness, Shed Excess Weight, and Help Your Body Fix Itself.* (New York: Harmony, 2015). p. 199.

Michael, Todd, MD. *The Twelve Conditions of a Miracle: The Miracle Worker's Handbook.* (New York: Tarcher/Penguin, 2004).

Moran, Victoria. *Creating a Charmed Life: Sensible, Spiritual Secrets Every Busy Woman Should Know.* (San Francisco: HarperSanFrancisco, 1999). p. 159.

Myss, Caroline, Ph.D. *Invisible Acts of Power: Personal Choices That Create Miracles.* (New York: Free Press, 2004). pp 269-270.

Nichols, Lisa. *Living Proof: Celebrating the Gifts that Came Wrapped in Sandpaper.* (no city: Yinspire media, 2011). p. 3.

Northrup, Christiane, M.D. *Goddesses Never Age: The Secret Prescription for Radiance, Vitality, and Well-Being.* (Carlsbad, CA: Hay House, 2015). pp. 299-325.

Orloff, Judith, M.D. *Second Sight.* (New York: Warner Books, 1996). p. 166.

Rankin, Lissa, M.D. *Mind Over Medicine: Scientific Proof That You Can Heal Yourself.* (Carlsbad, CA: Hay House, 2013). pp. 88-90.

Schaef, Anne Wilson. *Living in Process: Basic Truths for Living the Path of the Soul.* (New York: Ballantine Wellspring, 1998). p. 65.

Sommers, Suzanne. *Knockout: : Interviews with Doctors Who Are Curing Cancer—And How to Prevent Getting it in the First Place.* (New York: Harmony, 2009). p. 200.

Taylor, Sandra Anne. *Quantum Success: The Astounding Science of Wealth and Happiness.* (Carlsbad, CA: Hay House, 2006). pp. 200, 203-206.

Turner, John L., MD. *Medicine, Miracles, and Manifestations.* (Franklin Lakes, NJ: Career Press, 2009).

Turner, Kelly A., Ph.D. *Radical Remission: Surviving Cancer Against All Odds.* (New York: Harper One, 2014). pp. 217-253.

Walsch, Neale Donald. *Conversations with God: An Uncommon Dialogue (Book 2).* (Charlottesville, VA: Hampton Roads, 1997). p. 25

Williamson, Marianne. *The Gift of Change: Spiritual Guidance for a Radically New Life.* (San Francisco, CA: HarperSanFrancisco, 2004). p. 59.

PRAYER:

Arnot, Robert, M.D. *The Biology of Success.* (Boston: Little, Brown, 2000). pp. 193-199.

Braden, Gregg. *Secrets of the Lost Mode of Prayer: The Hidden Power of Beauty, Blessing, Wisdom, and Hurt.* (Carlsbad, CA: Hay House, 2006).

-----. *The Isaiah Effect: Decoding the Lost Science of Prayer and Prophecy.* (New York: Three Rivers Press, 2000). pp. 41, 145-173, 181, 208, 216, 241-242.

Byrne, Ronda. *The Secret.* (New York: Atria Books, 2006). pp. 151-152.

Das, Surya, Lama. *The Big Questions: How to Find Your Own Answers to Life's Essential Mysteries.* (New York: Rodale, 2007). pp. 77-78.

Dispenza, Joe, DC. *You Are the Placebo: Making Your Mind Matter.* (Carlsbad, CA: Hay House, 2014). p.299.

Dooley, Mike. *Even More Notes from the Universe: Dancing Life's Dance.* (New York: Atria Books, 2008). p. 20.

Dossey, Larry, M.D. *Healing Words: The Power of Prayer and the Practice of Medicine.* (New York: Harper One, 1994). pp. 57-108.

Eadie, Betty J. *The Awakening Heart: My Continuing Journey to Love.* (New York: Pocket Books, 1996). pp. 61, 121.

Eadie, Betty J. *Embraced by the Light.* (New York: Bantam, 1994).

Gikandi, David Cameron. *A Happy Pocket Full of Money: Your Quantum Leap into the Understanding, Having, and Enjoying Immense Wealth and Happiness.* (Bloomington, IN: Xlibris, 2008). p. 69.

Hay, Louise L. and Friends. *Gratitude: A Way of Life.* (Carlsbad, CA: Hay House, 1996). p. 128.

Khalsa, Dharma Singh, M.D. *Brain Longevity: The Breakthrough Medical Program that Improves Your Mind and Memory.* (New York: Warner Books, 1999). pp. 315-321.

Millman, Dan. *Living on Purpose: Straight Answers to Life's Tough Questions.* (Novato, CA: New World Library, 2000). p. 61.

Myss, Caroline, Ph.D. *Invisible Acts of Power: Personal Choices That Create Miracles.* (New York: Free Press, 2004). pp. 251, 279.

Northrup, Christiane, M.D. *Goddesses Never Age: The Secret Prescription for Radiance, Vitality, and Well-Being.* (Carlsbad, CA: Hay House, 2015). p. 319.

Warter, Carlos, M.D., Ph.D. *Recovery of the Sacred: Lessons in Soul Awareness.* (Deerfield Beach, FL: Health Communications, Inc., 1994). p. 5.

Williamson, Marianne. *Illuminata: A Return to Prayer.* (New York: Riverhead Books, 1994).

SURRENDER:

Moran, Victoria**.** *Creating a Charmed Like: Sensible, Spiritual Secrets Every Busy Woman Should Know.* (San Francisco: HarperSanFrancisco, 1999). pp. 22-25.

Taylor, Sandra Anne. *Quantum Success: The Astounding Science of Wealth and Happiness.* (Carlsbad, CA: Hay House, 2006). pp. 15, 24-25, 34.

Walsch, Neale Donald. *Conversations with God: An Uncommon Dialogue (Book 1).* (New York: Putnam, 1995). p. 104.

GRATITUDE:

Brett, Regina. *God Never Blinks: 50 Lessons for Life's Little Detours.* (New York: Grand Central Publishing, 2011).

Byrne, Rhonda. *The Magic.* (New York: Atria, 2012). p.19, 29, 31, 37, 111, 176.

-----. *The Secret.* (New York: Atria, 2006). p. 93.

Dyer, Wayne W., Ph.D. *The Power of Intention: Learning to Co-create Your World Your Way.* (Carlsbad, CA: Hay House, 2010.) pp. 153, 169, 260.

Dooley, Mike. *Manifesting Change: It Couldn't Be Easier.* (New York: Atria Books, 2010). p. 137

-----. *Notes from the Universe: New Perspectives from an Old Friend.* (New York: Atria Books, 2007). p. 52.

Emmons, Robert E., Ph.D. *Thanks: How the New Science of Gratitude Can Make You Happier.* (New York: Mariner Books/Houghton Mifflin/Harcourt, 2008). p. 87.

Emoto, Masaru, Ph.D. *The Hidden Messages in Water.* (Hillsboro, OR: Beyond Words Publishing, 2004). p. 81.

Hay, Louise L. and Friends. *Gratitude: A Way of Life.* (Carlsbad, CA: Hay House, 1996.) pp. 115, 175.

Katie, Byron. *A Thousand Names for Joy: Living in Harmony with the Way Things Are.* (New York: Three Rivers Press, 2007). p. 27.

Kralik, John, Judge. *365 Thank Yous: The Year a Simple Act of Daily Gratitude Changed My Life.* (New York: Hyperion: 2010).

Moran, Victoria. *Lit From Within: Tending Your Soul for Lifelong Beauty.* (San Francisco: HarperSanFrancisco, 2001). p. 227.

Northrup, Christiane, M.D. *Goddesses Never Age: The Secret Prescription for Radiance, Vitality, and Well-Being.* (Carlsbad, CA: Hay House, 2015). p. 319.

Norwood, Robin. *Why Me Why This Why Now: A Guide to Answering Life's Toughest Questions*: (New York: Tarcher, 2013, reprint). p. 169.

Rivers, Joan. *Don't Count the Candles: Just Keep the Fire Lit.* (New York: HarperCollins, 1999). p 67.

Taylor, Sandra Anne. *Quantum Success: The Astounding Science of Wealth and Happiness.* (Carlsbad, CA: Hay House, 2006). pp. 127, 153-161.

Thompson, L.D. *Fields of Plenty: A Guide to Your Inner Wisdom.* (Studio City, CA: Divine Arts, 2013). pp. 7-9.

Walsch, Neale Donald (2015, February 25). *I Believe God Wants You to Know.* Retrieved February 25, 2015 from today@nealedonaldwalsch.com

CELEBRATE:

Gattuso, Joan. *A Course in Life: The Twelve Universal Principles for Achieving a Life Beyond Your Dreams.* (New York: Tarcher/Putnam, 1998). pp. 100.

LaRoche, Loretta. *Life is Short—Wear Your Party Pants: Ten Simple Truths That Lead to an Amazing Life.* (Carlsbad, CA: Hay House, 2003). p. 8.

Nichols, Lisa. *Living Proof: Celebrating the Gifts That Come Wrapped in Sandpaper.* (America: Yinspire Media, 2011). p. 2.

Rasberry, Salli & Padi Selwyn. *Living Your Life Outloud: How to Unlock Your Creativity and Unleash Your Joy.* (New York: Pocket Books, 1995). pp. 47, 225.

Walsch, Neale Donald. *Conversations with God: An Uncommon Dialogue.* (Charlottesville, VA: Hampton Roads, 1998). p. 145.

Winter, Terrence P. "Castle (54, Ep7)." *Cops and Robbers.* Turner Network Television. TNT (037), 11 Mar. 2015. Television.

ENDNOTE:

Anderson, Greg. *Cancer: 50 Essential Things To Do.* (New York: Plume/Penguin, 2013). pp. 3-6.

Brett, Regina. *God Never Blinks: 50 Lessons for Life's Little Detours.* (New York: Grand Central Publishing, 2010). p. 147.

Burchard, Brendon. *The Charge: Activating the 10 Human Drives That Make You Feel Good.* New York: Free Press, 2012). pp. vii, 2.

Chodron, Pema. *When Things Fall Apart: Heart Advice for Difficult Times.* (Boston: Shambhala, 2000). p. 8.

Dooley, Mike. *The Top Ten Things Dead People Want to Tell You.* (Carlsbad, CA: Hay House, 2014). p. 36.

Keenan, Father Paul. *Good News for Bad Days: Living a Soulful Life.* (New York: Warner Books, 1998). p. 211.

Kubler-Ross, Elisabeth. *The Wheel of Life: A Memoir of Living and Dying.* (New York: Scribner, 1997). p. 193.

Norwood, Robin. *Why Me Why This Why Now: A Guide to Answering Life's Toughest Questions*: (New York: Tarcher, 2013). p. 169.

Pearl, Eric, Dr. & Frederick Ponzlov. *Solomon Speaks on Reconnecting Your Life.* (Carlsbad, CA: Hay House, 2013). pp. 123-125.

Siegel, Bernie S., M.D. *Love, Medicine, and Miracles: Lessons Learned About Self-Healing From a Surgeon's Experience with Exceptional Patients.* (New York: William Morrow, 1998). pp. x-xi.

Simonton, O. Carl, M.D., Stephanie Matthews-Simonton, & James L. Creighton. *Getting Well Again: A Step-by-Step Guide to Overcoming Cancer for Patients and their Families.* (New York: Bantam Books, Reissue 1992). pp. 105-106, 127-135.

Taylor, Sandra Anne. *Quantum Success: The Astounding Science of Wealth and Happiness*. (Carlsbad, CA: Hay House, 2006). pp. 61-62, 165-179.

Thompson, L.D. *Fields of Plenty: A Guide to Your Inner Wisdom*. (Studio City, CA: Divine Arts, 2013). pp. 203, 218.

There are 50 affirmations spread throughout these pages. They have been collected over the years. I have no idea where they all came from. Some I wrote. Some I have put my own spin on, and some are listed as found. As such, I offer my profound gratitude to those who may had originally written them. Thank you for sharing. —SLM

INDEX

C

D

E

F

G

H

I

J

K

L

M

N

O

T

U

V

W

Y

Z